W9-CKH-861

CENTRAL

973.04   Naff, Alixa
NAF
        The Arab Americans

DATE DUE

CENTRAL MIDDLE SCHOOL
MEDIA CENTER

The Arab Americans

Senior Consulting Editor

Senator Daniel Patrick Moynihan

Consulting Editors

Ann Orlov

Managing Editor, Harvard
Encyclopedia of American
Ethnic Groups

M. Mark Stolarik

*President, The Balch Institute
for Ethnic Studies, Philadelphia*

David M. Reimers

*Professor of History,
New York University*

James F. Watts

*Chairman, History Department,
City College of New York*

The

Arab
Americans

Alixa Naff

ARAB AMERICANS

973.04 NAF

9478

NAFF, ALIXA

CENTRAL MIDDLE MEDIA CENTER

CHELSEA HOUSE PUBLISHERS

Philadelphia

CENTRAL MIDDLE SCHOOL
MEDIA CENTER

CHELSEA HOUSE PUBLISHERS
Editor-in-Chief: Stephen Reginald
Production Manager: Pamela Loos
Art Director: Sara Davis
Picture Editor: Judy Hasday
Senior Production Editor: Lisa Chippendale

Staff for THE ARAB AMERICANS
Contributing Author: Tom Purdom
Production Editor: Nancy Lombardi
Cover Illustrator: Jane Sterrett

© 1999 by Chelsea House Publishers, a division of Main Line Book Co. All rights
reserved. Printed and bound in the United States of America.

First Printing
1   3   5   7   9   8   6   4   2

Library of Congress Cataloging-in-Publication Data
Naff, Alixa.
    The Arab Americans / Alixa Naff.
        p.   cm. — (The immigrant experience)
    Includes bibliographical references and index.
    Summary: Discusses the history, culture, and religion of the Arabs, factors encourag-
ing their emigration, and their acceptance as an ethnic group in North America.
    ISBN 0-7910-5051-3.
        0-7910-5053-X (pbk.)
    1. Arab Americans—Juvenile literature.   [1. Arab Americans.]   I. Title.
    II. Series.
E184.A65N34   1999
973′.04927—dc21   98-19612
                                                                  CIP
                                                                  AC

CONTENTS

THE IMMIGRANT EXPERIENCE

Other titles in preparation

CHELSEA HOUSE PUBLISHERS

A
NATION OF
NATIONS

Daniel Patrick Moynihan

The Constitution of the United States begins: "We the People of the United States. . . ." Yet, as we know, the United States was not then and is not now made up of a single group of people. It is made up of many peoples. Immigrants and bondsmen from Europe, Asia, Africa, and Central and South America came here or were brought here, and still they come. They forged one nation and made it their own. More than 100 years ago, Walt Whitman expressed this great central fact of America: "Here is not merely a nation, but a teeming Nation of nations."

Although the ingenuity and acts of courage of these immigrants, our ancestors, shaped the North American way of life, we sometimes take their contributions for granted. This fine series, *The Immigrant Experience*, examines the experiences and contributions of different immigrant groups and how these contributions determined the future of the United States and Canada.

Immigrants did not abandon their ethnic traditions when they reached the shores of North America. Each ethnic group had its own customs and traditions, and each brought different experiences, accomplishments, skills, values, styles of dress, and tastes in food that lingered long after its arrival. Yet this profusion of differences created a singularity, or bond, among the immigrants.

The United States and Canada are unusual in this respect. Whereas religious and ethnic differences have sparked intolerance throughout the rest of the world—from the 17th-century religious wars to the 19th-century nationalist movements in Europe to the near extermination of the Jewish people under Nazi Germany—North Americans have struggled to learn how to respect each other's differences and live in harmony.

Our two countries are hardly the only two in which different groups must learn to live together. There is no nation of significant size anywhere in the world which would not be classified as multiethnic. But only in North America are there so *many* different groups, most of them living cheek by jowl with one another.

This is not easy. Look around the world. And it has not always been easy for us. Witness the exclusion of Chinese immigrants, and for practical purposes Japanese also, in the late 19th century. But by the late 20th century, Chinese and Japanese Americans were the most successful of all the groups recorded by the census. We have had prejudice aplenty, but it has been resisted and recurrently overcome.

The remarkable ability of Americans to live together as one people was seriously threatened by the issue of slavery. Thousands of settlers from the British Isles had arrived in the colonies as indentured servants, agreeing to work for a specified number of years on farms or as apprentices in return for passage to America and room and board. When the first Africans arrived in the then-British colonies during the 17th century, some colonists thought that they too should be treated as indentured servants. Eventually, the question of whether the Africans should be treated as indentured, like the English, or as slaves who could be owned for life was considered in a Maryland court. The court's calamitous decree held that blacks were slaves bound to a lifelong servitude, and so also were their children. America went through a time of moral examination and civil war before it finally freed African slaves and their descendants. The principle that all people are created equal had faced its greatest challenge and survived.

Yet the court ruling that set blacks apart from other races fanned flames of discrimination that burned long after slavery was abolished—and that still flicker today. Indeed, it was about the time of the American Civil War that European theories of evolution were turned to the service of ranking different peoples by their presumed distance from our apelike ancestors.

When the Irish flooded American cities to escape the famine in Ireland, the cartoonists caricatured the typical "Paddy" (a common term for Irish immigrants) as an apelike creature with jutting jaw and sloping forehead.

By the 20th century, racism and ethnic prejudice had given rise to virulent theories of a Northern European master race. When Adolf Hitler came to power in Germany in 1933, he popularized the notion of an Aryan race. Only a man of the deepest ignorance and evil could have done this. *Aryan* is a Sanskrit word, which is to say the ancient script of what we now think of as India. It means "noble" and was adopted by linguists—notably by a fine German scholar, Max Müller—to denote the Indo-European family of languages. Müller was horrified that anyone could think of it in terms of race, especially a race of blond-haired, blue-eyed Teutons. But the Nazis embraced the notion of a master race. Anyone with darker and heavier features was considered inferior. Buttressed by these theories, the German Nazi state from 1933 to 1945 set out to destroy European Jews, along with Poles, Gypsies, Russians, and other groups considered inferior. It nearly succeeded. Millions of these people were murdered.

The tragedies brought on by ethnic and racial intolerance throughout the world demonstrate the importance of North America's efforts to create a society free of prejudice and inequality.

A relatively recent example of the New World's desire to resolve ethnic friction nonviolently is the solution that the Canadians found to a conflict between two ethnic groups. A longstanding dispute as to whether Canadian culture was properly

English or French resurfaced in the mid-1960s, dividing the peoples of the French-speaking Province of Quebec from those of the English-speaking provinces. Relations grew tense, then bitter, then violent. The Royal Commission on Bilingualism and Biculturalism was established to study the growing crisis and to propose measures to ease the tensions. As a result of the commission's recommendations, all official documents and statements from the national government's capital at Ottawa are now issued in both French and English, and bilingual education is encouraged.

The year 1980 marked a coming of age for the United States's ethnic heritage. For the first time, the U.S. Bureau of the Census asked people about their ethnic background. Americans chose from more than 100 groups, including French Basque, Spanish Basque, French Canadian, African American, Peruvian, Armenian, Chinese, and Japanese. The ethnic group with the largest response was English (49.6 million). More than 100 million Americans claimed ancestors from the British Isles, which includes England, Ireland, Wales, and Scotland. There were almost as many Germans (49.2 million) as English. The Irish-American population (40.2 million) was third, but the next-largest ethnic group, the African Americans, was a distant fourth (21 million). There was a sizable group of French ancestry (13 million) as well as of Italian (12 million). Poles, Dutch, Swedes, Norwegians, and Russians followed. These groups, and other smaller ones, represent the wondrous profusion of ethnic influences in North America.

Canada too has learned more about the diversity of its population. Studies conducted during the French/English conflict showed that Canadians were descended from Ukrainians, Germans, Italians, Chinese, Japanese, native Indians, and Inuit, among others. Canada found it had no ethnic majority, although nearly half of its immigrant population had come from the British Isles. Canada, like the United States, is a land of immigrants for whom mutual tolerance is a matter of reason as well as principle. But note how difficult this can be in practice, even for persons of manifest goodwill.

The people of North America are the descendants of one of the greatest migrations in history. And that migration is not over. Koreans, Vietnamese, Nicaraguans, Cubans, and many others are heading for the shores of North America in large numbers. This mix of cultures shapes every aspect of our lives. To understand ourselves, we must know something about our diverse ethnic ancestry. Nothing so defines the North American nations as the motto on the Great Seal of the United States: *E Pluribus Unum*—Out of Many, One.

Syrian immigrants and their American-born children adapted easily to life in the New World.

Out of Arab Lands

The Arabs are made up of several different peoples who live in North Africa and western Asia (the Middle East) and share a common culture. They speak Arabic, a Semitic language that originated in the Arabian Peninsula, and most practice Islam, although a number are Christians. When Islam, the religion founded by Muhammad, spread throughout the Middle East during the 7th century, it united the people of the region into one of the world's great civilizations. But the notion of Arab political unity and the practice of identifying an Arabic-speaking person as an "Arab" rather than as a member of a family, village, or religious sect dates only from the early part of the 20th century.

The modern Arab world consists of Algeria, Bahrain, Egypt, Iraq, Jordan, Kuwait, Lebanon, Libya, Morocco, Oman, Qatar, Saudi Arabia, Sudan, Syria, Tunisia, the United Arab Emirates, and Yemen. It also includes the territories known as the Gaza Strip and the West Bank, where Palestinians are working to build a state of their own, independent of Israel. From all these parts of the Arab world, immigrants in search of opportunity have migrated to North America. Their descendants have a heritage rich in the traditions of both the old world and the new.

The United States counts approximately 2 million Arab Americans among its citizens, but any estimation of the size of the current Arab American population is at best imprecise. About half descend from immigrants who came to America between 1880 and 1940 and half

13

from those who arrived after World War II. During both periods immigration officials have had difficulty in classifying Arabs accurately. Because those who immigrated before World War II were Ottoman subjects immigration officials frequently registered them inaccurately, along with Turks and Armenians, as being from "Turkey in Asia."

Not until 1899 did the designation "Syrian" appear on immigration rolls, and the term *Palestinian* entered use even later. More recently, Arab immigrants have often been registered according to their last country of residence, which also causes confusion. In 1948, with the creation of Israel in Palestine, Palestinians lost official recognition of their nationality. They came to North America from the various Arab countries to which they were displaced and were listed as citizens of those countries. Arab immigrants including Palestinians can still receive the imprecise classification "other Asian" or "other African."

The first great wave of Arab immigration to North America took place before World War I, when thousands emigrated from the Syrian province of the Ottoman Empire. Most of these first immigrants, about 90 percent of whom were Christian, came from Mt. Lebanon, a semiautonomous Syrian district on the Mediterranean's eastern shore. Poor farmers of the region had heard of the money they could make as itinerant peddlers. They came intending to stay in the United States only temporarily, hoping to make their fortunes and to return to their native villages where they could lead lives of relative ease. Few, in fact, returned to their homeland.

Syrian peddlers thrived in America. They saw no reason to leave and soon made a new life for themselves. As they peddled their way across the continent, they learned American ways and amassed substantial savings, which they later invested in family-owned businesses. In their eagerness to join the country's rising middle class, these Syrian Americans soon became more American than Syrian.

The second great wave of Arab immigration followed World War II, which had led to the formation of the Jewish state of Israel and several newly independent Arab nations in the Middle East. Like their predecessors, many of these later immigrants also intended to stay only a short while. Some sought refuge from political and military turmoil that they thought would end soon, some came to study or to reap the benefits of their college educations. Many were professionals—lawyers, doctors, engineers—with limited opportunities in their underdeveloped homelands. They planned to make enough money in North America to return and live comfortably in the Middle East.

Recent Arab immigrants blend easily into American society, although in contrast to their first-wave counterparts, most practice Islam and all come from nationalistic Arab states. Most retain strong feelings of solidarity with their troubled homelands, especially after Israel's humiliating defeat of the Arabs in the 1967 Arab–Israeli War. Since then, many Americanized descendants of the early Syrian immigrants have adopted the nationalistic pride of the more recent arrivals. The two groups of Arab Americans thus share concern for the Middle-East situation and its effects on their lives in the New World.

Even though most are both economically and culturally assimilated, Arab Americans work together today to encourage improved relations between the United States and the Arab states. Worried by growing anti-Arab discrimination, they are uniting to promote understanding between themselves and other Americans. Their heightened political consciousness has also motivated many Arab Americans to rediscover their ancestral language and culture, at the same time that they remain proud Americans.

From antiquity to the present, caravan traders have figured in the history of Arab lands.

MANY HOMELANDS, ONE PEOPLE

Diversity more than unity characterizes the Arab world. The Arabs live in part of the region known as the Middle East, in an area which extends from Morocco to Egypt and Sudan in North Africa and from Syria and Iraq in western Asia to Yemen and Oman in the Arabian Peninsula. This area includes vast deserts and formidable mountain ranges as well as arid steppes and fertile river valleys. No less varied than the geography of their homeland, the Arab people differ from one another racially, religiously, ethnically, historically, and politically. Nevertheless, they share a common language and heritage. Islam, the religion practiced by the overwhelming majority of Arabs, lends even greater coherence to their culture.

Climate and geography have contributed much to the heterogeneity of the Arab nations. The scarcity of fresh water in many regions, for instance, has caused some Arabs to become nomadic bedouin and others to become ingenious farmers. Bedouin herd sheep, goats, and camels from one pasture to the next in the perpetual search for water, while farming villagers in dry areas have developed sophisticated irrigation methods that have allowed them to survive in an arid climate. Other Arabs live in well-watered mountain and coastal regions

CENTRAL MIDDLE SCHOOL
MEDIA CENTER

Centuries before the birth of Christ, sophisticated civilizations thrived on the Arabian Peninsula. This frieze is from the 6th century B.C.

where crops are abundant. Because Arab lands are surrounded by great bodies of water—the Atlantic Ocean, the Mediterranean, Arabian, and Red seas, and the Persian Gulf—fishing villages flourish along the coasts.

At the same time, the port and inland cities of the Arab world support merchants and artisans of every description. In ancient times, land and water routes converged in the centrally located Middle East, making it hospitable to caravan traders, as well. In the 20th century, the Arabian Peninsula's oil reserves (an estimated two thirds of the world's total) brought tremendous prosperity and rapid modernization to the countries there.

Outsiders have played a major role in the history of the Arab world and the development of its culture. The lands of southwest Asia lie at the crossroads of historically important trade routes linking Asia, Africa, and Europe. These trade routes helped create great commercial cities, such as Aleppo, Damascus, and Cairo, that have long served as centers for the exchange of ideas, news, and commodities. North African Arab lands, on the other hand, lie close to European and African nations, and the people there have absorbed diverse cultural influences from their neighbors.

Drawn by the wealth offered by trade, the world's most powerful empires—including ancient Egypt, Rome, and more recently Ottoman Turkey and Europe—have dominated the region for most of its history. Though Arab nations gained independence during the 20th century, the United States and the Soviet Union struggled for influence in the Middle East throughout the Cold War. Today, the region is still a frequent source of international disagreements.

The history of the Arab world starts with the dawn of civilization. Archaeologists believe that the earliest humans may have lived in the Fertile Crescent—a curve of rich, well-watered land south of the Syrian desert and north of the Arabian Peninsula and extending from the southeastern coast of the Mediterranean Sea to the Persian Gulf. The first mention of Arabs in ancient historical records occurs around 1000 B.C. At that time the Arabs inhabited a few prosperous cities and small settlements and wandered the desert as nomads in the Arabian Peninsula. They spoke Arabic—a Semitic language—and claimed to have descended from the Semitic patriarch Abraham (through his son Ishmael) or Noah (through his grandson Joktan).

During pre-Christian and early Christian times, other Semitic civilizations such as the Hebrews, Babylonians, Assyrians, and Phoenicians and great non-Semitic cultures such as ancient Egypt, Persia, Rome, Macedonia, and Greece conquered various parts of the Middle East and North Africa, including the Arabian Peninsula. By the 6th century, overrun again and again by outsiders, the tribes of the Arabian Peninsula had entered a period of decline. Only with the birth of Islam did the Arabs rise, ultimately to become a mighty empire.

A New Religion

Two other great monotheistic religions (based on a belief in a single god)—Judaism and Christianity—had been practiced in the Middle East for centuries when, in about A.D. 570, the Arab prophet Muhammad was born in Mecca, a city on the Arabian Peninsula. In the early 7th century, Muhammad's teachings became the basis of Islam, which claimed to fulfill the prophecies of Judaism and Christianity. In Islamic belief, Muhammad, the greatest prophet, completes a line of prophets starting with Adam and continuing through Moses to Jesus.

As the successor to Judaism and Christianity, Islam incorporates many of the beliefs and practices of the older religions. In fact, *Islam* translates as "submission to one all-powerful God," the same God worshiped by Jews and Christians. Out of respect for its origins, Islam required its adherents to be tolerant of Jews and Christians. Nonetheless, in its earliest days Islam was a distinctly Arab religion, inextricably joined to Arabic culture and language.

The followers of Islam are called Muslims. They believe that *Allah* (God) sent Muhammad to warn humanity of the consequences of its evil ways. Allah's message, as delivered to Muhammad by the angel Gabriel, is recorded in Arabic in the *Quran*, the Islamic holy book. The Quran (or Koran) contains teachings upon which Muslims base their Holy Law, or *Shari'a*, covering many aspects of believers' everyday life. In accordance with Holy Law, for instance, Muslims keep the Sabbath on Friday and do not eat pork or drink alcoholic beverages. The Shari'a also touches on civil, personal, criminal, and inheritance issues not dealt with in the Quran itself. Much like orthodox Jews, who also subscribe to a rigorous Holy Law, Muslims practice their religion best in a society organized according to the Shari'a. They do not distinguish between religious beliefs and social mores; indeed, Muslims feel that fol-

The prophet Muhammad brought Islam to the Arab peoples, who then spread his word throughout North Africa and western Asia.

lowing the Holy Law is more important than performing their religious rituals. As a result, many Islamic Arab nations have governments based on the Shari'a.

The Shari'a also requires all Muslims to fulfill the "five pillars of the faith." The first pillar, the profession of faith, involves stating and believing the words "There is no God but the One God and Muhammad is His Messenger." The second pillar directs believers to bow in prayer toward the holy city of Mecca five times a day. According to the third, Muslims must give alms to the poor and needy. The fourth pillar requires fasting during the daylight hours throughout the holy month of Ramadan, the ninth month of the Muslim calendar, during which Muhammad received his first revelation from God. To fulfill the fifth pillar, Muslims must make a pilgrimage to Mecca at least once in their lifetime.

In the course of its history, Islam has split into several sects. Sunnites, the largest group; Shi'ites, the next largest; and other smaller groups disagreed about the identity of Muhammad's rightful successor and other theological questions. In the 11th century another sect, the Druze, broke away from the Shi'ites. The Druze accept many Islamic teachings but do not necessarily observe the five pillars of faith. Instead, they have formulated other beliefs and practices, recorded in *al-*

Muslims observe the fifth pillar of faith by completing a pilgrimage to Mecca, Muhammad's birthplace. Here, believers gather at the Kaaba, the inner sanctuary of the Great Mosque.

The "Arabicized" peoples of the Islamic empire advanced scientific and mathematical knowledge, writing treatises on such subjects as automata. This illustration depicts a mechanical toy in the form of a boat.

Hikma, a holy book of their own. Many Druze consider themselves semi-Islamic, others consider their religion to be entirely separate.

Once the occupants of the Arabian Peninsula had adopted Islam, the history of the Arabs became, to a great extent, the history of Islam. Islamic law permeated every aspect of Arab life. Sunnite religious leaders, referred to as *caliphs*, ruled the Arab nations and sought to expand the Islamic empire. The centuries that followed saw the spread of Islam throughout the Middle East. Along with Islam, the Arabic language and culture also came to dominate the region.

The Arab Empire

In A.D. 632 Muhammad died. Inspired by zeal for their new religion, Muslims rode out of the Arabian Peninsula on horseback to carry their beliefs to the rest of the known world. During the next hundred years, Arab armies conquered peoples of diverse cultures and languages and dominated the region stretching from the borders of China and India in the east to North Africa and Spain in the west. The conquering Muslims converted most of their new subjects to Islam and in many cases absorbed them into their tribes. Throughout

North Africa and western Asia, converts to Islam learned the Arabic language. Even Christians and Jews who did not accept Islam soon spoke Arabic and adopted Arab customs.

Rather than destroy those whom they conquered, the Arabs followed the Islamic law of tolerance. They integrated with non-Arab peoples, and a dynamic, sophisticated new Arab culture evolved. Drawing on the rich heritage of other nations—Persia, Byzantium, and India in particular—the Arab Empire grew into one of the world's great civilizations. Between the 7th and 12th centuries, Arabs made extraordinary contributions to the fields of architecture, music, art, literature, science, and philosophy.

Arabs translated and preserved the manuscripts of the ancient Greek philosophers and the writings of the great thinkers of Christian Byzantium (previously the eastern portion of the Roman Empire). Their accomplishments in mathematics included the development of algebra and the arabic numeral system used today. Arab scientists invented the mariner's compass and the astrolabe (used to calculate the positions of stars and planets) and made tremendous advances in medicine and agriculture.

Arab intellectuals formulated sophisticated concepts of municipal administration, commerce, and measurement and wrote major philosophical, geographic, and

The Arab empire spread as far west as Spain, where its influence is still visible in elaborate Moorish architecture.

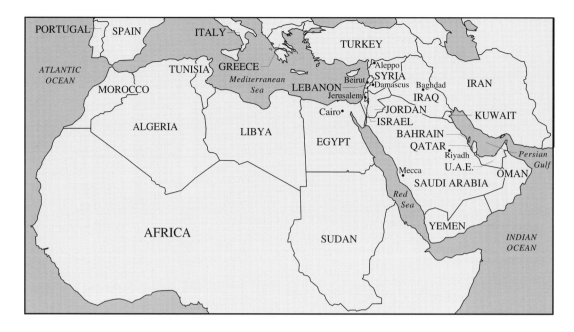

historical treatises. The decorative arts flourished, and writers produced an enormous body of literature, including beautiful poetry and the classic prose work *Arabian Nights* (or *The Thousand and One Nights*). In the 9th and 10th centuries, the golden age of the Arab Empire, Muslim cities such as Baghdad (Iraq), Cairo (Egypt), and Cordoba (Spain) ranked among the world's major centers of learning and culture.

During this period of expansion and prosperity, the Islamic caliphs ruled a united empire, but by the end of the 10th century a period of political fragmentation had begun. In subsequent centuries, the Christian Crusaders from Europe and the Mongols from Asia captured Arab lands. Islamic civilization declined, and in the 16th century the Ottoman Turks conquered the Arab lands from Syria to Morocco, though they did not take the Arabian Peninsula. Proud Arab peoples became mere subjects of the Ottoman Empire. Over the next 400 years the Ottoman Empire held sway in the Middle East. But it started to weaken in the 17th century and Europeans gained influence in the region. Yet the reign of the Turks did not end until World War I, when they suffered defeat alongside their German allies.

European Influence

From 1830 to 1918, as the Ottoman Empire decayed and crumbled, Arab lands (with the exception of what is now Saudi Arabia and northwestern Yemen) gradually came under British and French influence. The Ottoman court retained nominal control of some regions, but France and Britain, in competition with Russia and Austria-Hungary, eventually gained a foothold in North Africa and the Middle East. During the struggle, the European powers fought to gain the loyalty of the various Arab Christian sects, thus deepening the divisions between religious groups. By favoring the Christian minority over the Muslim majority, the Europeans kindled hostility between the two religions and disrupted the centuries-old accommodation between them. The turmoil limited the Arabs' ability to act in their own interest.

At the same time, the United States began to play a role in some parts of the Middle East. In Mt. Lebanon and Syria the American Protestant Mission opened schools and churches that taught children some Arabic and English as well as history and mathematics. American missionaries published a new Arabic translation of the Bible and produced secular textbooks on grammar, algebra, geometry, and geography. Their most lasting contribution came with the founding of the Syrian Protestant College (now the American University in Beirut). The American Protestants also provided food and medical assistance during periods of strife in the region.

The era remained one of Ottoman rule, however. When World War I broke out and the Ottomans, hoping to put an end to British and French influence in their territory, entered on the side of the Germans, some Arabs saw an opportunity to work toward establishing an independent Arab state. They provided Britain with military assistance in return for promises that the British would help them set up an autonomous Arab nation once the war was won. Britain and the other Allied forces—including France, Russia, and the

During the 400-year reign of the Ottoman Turks, European missionaries were sent to the Middle East to run schools for native children.

United States—defeated Germany, and the Ottoman Empire collapsed. Power over the region fell to France and Britain, but England betrayed its promise to the Arabs. Without regard to the wishes of the Arabs, Britain and France changed the map of the Middle East. And in the Balfour Declaration of 1917, Britain supported Jewish wishes to establish a homeland for themselves in Palestine.

France was equally disdainful of Arab interests. It deposed the British-installed Syrian king in 1920, occupied the country, and carved Greater Lebanon out of Syrian lands, leaving Syria with only one port. The French later ceded another Syrian province to the new Republic of Turkey. England took another piece of Syria to create Transjordan (now the kingdom of Jordan), reserved Palestine for the future creation of a Jewish state, and unified several former Ottoman provinces into Iraq. In addition, France and Britain continued to control territories in which they had interfered since the 19th century. The actions of the European powers inspired a new Arab nationalism with a strong anti-Western slant.

Arab Independence and the Jewish Homeland

World War II brought an end to colonial rule (except in Egypt and Algeria, which did not win independence until 1953 and 1962, respectively). This group of independent states was soon referred to as the Arab world. In 1947, however, the United Nations, including the United States and the Soviet Union, voted to par-

After World War II, European Jews rushed to Palestine to live in a Jewish homeland.

Palestinian Arabs were forced into refugee camps when their lands became Jewish property.

tition Palestine into Arab and Jewish states. The Jews traced their claim on this territory back to the biblical kingdoms of Israel and Judah, though few Jews had lived there from the time of Jerusalem's fall to Rome in A.D. 70 until the start of Jewish settlement in the late 19th century. Other peoples indigenous to Palestine, who were Arabicized during the Islamic expansion, had lived in the region throughout history. Both Christians and Muslims hold many locations there to be sacred, and the Palestinian Arabs felt the land was rightfully theirs.

In the early 20th century, European Jews flooded into the territory. In 1948, Israel declared itself a state, hundreds of thousands of Arabs fled, and fighting started. Fifty-five non-Arab nations officially recognized Israel's statehood, the UN intervened in the Arab-Israeli conflict, and within a year the fighting ended. Since then, however, the Middle East has experienced intermittent warfare and constant political tension.

In 1956, Israel, together with Britain and France, attacked Egypt. The intervention of the UN quickly ended that struggle, but other conflicts persisted, and in 1967 war broke out between Israel, Syria, and Egypt. Israel soundly defeated its foes in the Six-Day War and occupied Arab territories then inhabited by about a million Arabs. Jews founded settlements in the occupied territories, while many Palestinians remained in refugee camps outside their former homeland. Another war erupted between Israel and its neighbors in 1973. In 1979, Israel and Egypt signed a formal peace treaty, but Israel's hostilities with other Arab states continued.

In 1975, civil war broke out in Lebanon. Israel and Syria both invaded Lebanon, and they continued to occupy parts of the country when the war ended in 1990. Meanwhile, Iraq spent most of the 1980s fighting a devastating war with Iran (not an Arab country). Then, in 1990, Iraq invaded Kuwait, prompting a U.S.–led military operation to expel the Iraqis in 1991. On a more hopeful note, the 1990s brought negotiations between the Palestinians and the Israelis that resulted in the first steps toward a self-governing Palestinian state. All these political struggles gain international significance from the region's strategic location and its importance as the world's primary source of oil.

Since the 1960s, the development of the Arab world's oil reserves has had a profound impact on the region's economy. The countries of the Arabian Peninsula, particularly Saudi Arabia and Kuwait, have grown from relatively poor countries that supported farming and nomadic populations into a wealthy, influ-

Countries all over the world soon recognized Israeli sovereignty. Shown here, the United Nations vote to admit the new state to its membership.

ential group of nations. Their economies have flourished, their urban centers have expanded rapidly, and some governments now support sophisticated welfare and defense systems. But the economic gap has widened between the oil states and those without significant oil reserves. Although millions of Arabs have entered a new age of prosperity, this disparity may contribute further to the region's instability.

Throughout its history, the Arab world has undergone many changes, yet Islam and Arab culture have endured. The Arabs have always had to work hard to draw a modest living from their reluctant lands, but they have seldom starved. They have alternately dominated and been subject to many different empires and have—until the formation of Israel—assimilated rather than rejected these diverse civilizations. This tendency to integrate rather than reject or destroy other cultures has allowed the Arabs to thrive and to develop a rich heritage of their own. As fellow Muslims, for instance, the Ottoman Turks did not try to destroy Arab culture. Only the European states that colonized the region and later partitioned Palestine posed a real threat to the Arab world. ∾

Palestinians proudly display their flag during a pro-peace parade to show support for the on-going negotiations for a self-governing Palestinian state.

Like most immigrants, this Syrian in traditional dress probably intended to return home to Mt. Lebanon within a few years, after making his fortune in "Amrika."

On the Move

Some historians argue that Arabs first came to America from Moorish Spain, arriving with Christopher Columbus in 1492. The great wave of Arab immigration to the United States, however, did not start until the late 1800s. It lasted until 1924, halting briefly during World War I. About 90 percent of the Arab immigrants came to America from the Mt. Lebanon district of Syria, a predominantly Christian province of the Ottoman Empire on the eastern shore of the Mediterranean. The others came mostly from Palestine.

Two significant factors contributed to Mt. Lebanon's early role as the center of immigration from the Middle East. Those wishing to leave semiautonomous Mt. Lebanon found it easier to dodge Ottoman restrictions on immigration than did Arabs from other areas. In addition, the Christian Arabs of Mt. Lebanon did not share many of the fears Muslims had about living in a Christian land, so more of them felt inclined to try their luck in "Amrika."

Unlike other ethnic groups, many of whom migrated to North America to escape famine and oppression, most Syrian immigrants to the United States and Canada had no reason to come other than better opportunity. Arab Christians may have resented Muslim rule, but between 1861 and 1915 (which included the period of the greatest migration) Mt. Lebanon enjoyed both prosperity and political stability. Nonetheless, Syrians saw the chance to get rich in the New World. They planned to "pluck the gold from the trees" and return to Syria a year or two later to enjoy a life of comfort and enhanced status.

Devout Muslims, fiercely loyal to their tribes, bedouin nomads rarely left their homeland.

Heartened by the stories of success told by early Christian immigrants, Muslim and Druze Syrians later made the trek to America, although their numbers never accounted for more than 10 percent of the Syrian total. The first of these immigrants sent encouraging letters to their friends and families back home, and many Muslims and Druze soon overcame their fear that life in a Christian country would interfere with their religious practices. After 1908, in addition to the economic motivations they shared with Christian Arabs, Muslim and Druze men had a particularly compelling reason to emigrate: The Ottoman government drafted Muslim Arabs into the Turkish army, and a number of young men emigrated to escape military service.

Between 1880 and 1914, an estimated 100,000 Syrians left their homeland for America. Most of the emigrants had farmed small, disconnected plots of land and supplemented their incomes through trade or craft work. Intellectuals and professionals represented only a small group, but a surprisingly large percentage of the immigrants consisted of Christian women traveling alone. Some came to America to join husbands or fiancés, but many came simply to earn money, and some even left husbands behind. As Arab men and women established themselves in the New World, they sent for their families from overseas. World War I temporarily interrupted the flow of immigration, but as soon as the opportunity arose, many Syrians who survived wartime famine fled. More left when the Allied forces divided the fallen Ottoman Empire between them, in effect colonizing most of the Middle East. Between 1920 and 1924 more than 12,000 Syrians arrived in America, but the Johnson-Reed Immigration Act of 1924, which set quotas for immigration to the United States, limited Syrian immigration to 100 people per year, terminating the great migration. By 1940, however, at least 206,000 Syrian Americans (either foreign-born or American-born) lived in the United States.

Discovering "Amrika"

The Ottoman sultan may have unwittingly sparked Arab migration in 1876 when he asked his subjects to exhibit their traditional arts and crafts at the Philadelphia Centennial Exposition. This event, a celebration of America's centennial, included exhibits from all over the world. A handful of merchants and artisans from Syria (and perhaps also from Palestine) heeded the sultan's call. They brought their wares to the exposition and got their first taste of American prosperity. Excited by what they found, they sent enthusiastic letters back home. Hundreds of Arabs, hoping to make their fortunes, followed these trailblazers to America.

When some of the early adventurers returned home for visits sporting Western suits, felt fedoras, polished leather shoes, and gold watch fobs, they presented themselves as living proof that immigrants could find instant wealth in America. Most had indeed succeeded—as pack peddlers who carried their wares from town to town on their backs. A few others had found work in booming new American industries. Their tales of money inspired hundreds of ambitious young men and women, especially those from farms and villages, to make the trip. By the 1890s, groups of up to 200 people from single towns or villages traveled to the New World together.

The memoirs of these early immigrants reveal their great expectations as they packed their bags for America. In 1895, at the age of 19, Faris N. (initials used in place of surnames to protect the privacy of those quoted) visited three cousins who had just come back from the United States. "I asked them about work there," Faris wrote in his memoirs. "They said it was in trading and one could make three English pounds which is about $15.00. I said, 'Three English pounds!' . . . Then I returned home and said, 'Mama, what do you think? I want to go to America and I will be away from you for two years.' " Within a few weeks, Faris

had left with 32 others from his village. Like so many others, he stayed in the New World.

Mike H. recalled that in 1892 one of his village's poorest families had written from America that they had earned enough to save $800. "All of my village of Ayn Arab rushed to America," Mike wrote. "It was like a gold rush." He, along with 72 others, left in 1895.

The Turks soon felt threatened by the mass migration, which was draining the Syrian labor force and depriving the government of an important source of revenue. They tried to keep the Syrians home, but with little success. Even when military police guarded roads

In 1876 Syrian subjects of the Ottoman Empire exhibited their native arts and crafts in the Turkish Pavilion at the Centennial Exhibition in Philadelphia.

and ports, the Syrians bribed Turkish officials or escaped in dinghies to the big ships. "We hid in the woods for over eight hours before we could leave at night," wrote Elizabeth B. Undaunted by the barriers to emigration, thousands of Syrians decided that they would make it to America, one way or another.

Journey to the New World

To finance the trip to America, most families had to dig deep into their savings, and some even mortgaged the family land. But they made such sacrifices willingly, and those who remained behind always made sure the traveler took along a little extra pocket money as insurance against misfortune. Syrian families considered the expense of sending members to America an investment: If one of them struck it rich, the whole family would share in the bounty. As time went on, the flow of money reversed. Immigrants prospering as peddlers in the United States sent remittances home and paid the passage for their families to come and join them.

Rumors of easy wealth tempted struggling Syrian farmers and laborers to try their luck in the New World.

Like millions of other immigrants before World War I, Syrians traveled in steerage. Crowded like cattle onto ships, they patiently endured stench, filth, and sleepless nights during their journey. Their dreams of America helped distract them from shipboard conditions. Most of these provincial Arabs had never ventured far from their villages, spoke little or no English, and knew nothing about America's geography, climate, or customs. They whiled away the hours of their long, unpleasant voyage wondering what they would find when they landed at Ellis Island. Would their relatives meet them there? Would they get through inspection or be turned away? What was America really like? On board, they waited impatiently to reach New York, the port of entry, where a thriving Syrian colony awaited them in lower Manhattan. Many immigrants paused there for rest and assistance before traveling on to other destinations.

Some Syrian immigrants never arrived in New York at all, although they expected to. Greedy or misinformed steamship agents and travel brokers often misrouted passengers, booking them on ships destined for other U.S. ports or for Canada, South or Central America, the Caribbean, or even Australia. Unscrupulous agents led their unsuspecting clients to believe that they would arrive in New York within a few weeks. But instead, these immigrants would land six months later in such places as Brazil or Australia, thinking they had reached American soil. When they discovered that they had been duped, most shrugged their shoulders and settled wherever they had ended up, although some struggled on for months more in order to reach their families in the United States.

A Generation of Peddlers

The Syrians who arrived in the United States around the turn of the century did not share many characteristics with other, larger groups of newcomers. Their traditional clothing and olive skin set them apart from northern and western European immigrants, as did their language, customs, and some of their values. Syrians differed in another way from typical foreigners who came to the United States: Few of them joined the rapidly growing industrial labor force. Although some Syrians did take factory jobs, the vast majority worked as pack peddlers, selling their wares from farm to farm or town to town.

This choice had a profound effect on the experience of Syrians in the United States. Peddling took them into the homes of Americans, enabling them to learn the language and customs of their adopted country. As itinerant workers based in peddling settlements, they also avoided the ghetto ordeal and cultural isolation that plagued so many immigrant communities.

Other ethnic groups also worked as peddlers, but the Syrians identified themselves most thoroughly with the trade. Groups from Mt. Lebanon left their native villages to peddle all over the United States, even in Alaska. If they happened to land in Canada, Mexico, or some other unforeseen location, they peddled there with the same vigor, frequently crossing borders to find new customers. And although they began pack peddling at a time when new methods of communication, transportation, and selling threatened their industry with extinction, most Syrian peddlers succeeded, and many made a small fortune.

Life on the road involved hardships that some early Syrian immigrants considered too difficult or degrading to be worth the money, but most Syrians preferred the independence of peddling to the drudgery of factory work or the isolation of farming. Peddling required no money, training, or knowledge of English; it suited the independent Syrian nature; and it offered the possibility of earning a great deal of money in a relatively short period of time. Peddlers were also spared the uncertainty of finding factory work, the long hours of waiting in line for jobs, and the frequent layoffs suffered by unskilled industrial laborers.

Syrian peddlers usually began their lives in America by seeking out a Syrian supplier they knew or had heard about. Suppliers, friendly faces in an unfamiliar land, represented a link between the old and the new. Veteran peddlers who had accumulated some savings and were ready to lay down their packs often became suppliers. They generally set up shop in small towns or cities with railroad stops and vigorous economies. Many suppliers actively recruited immigrants from Syria, sending for relatives and friends from their native villages. As family members and people from the same villages joined earlier immigrants, peddling settlements grew up around the suppliers.

Immigrants from the Middle East, who came from a culture vastly different from that of the New World, stood out from the crowds of European arrivals.

In the late 19th and early 20th centuries, carrying heavy packs on their backs, Syrian peddlers in North America walked countless miles on country roads in all kinds of weather.

One such supplier was Nick R., who came to New York in 1887 and peddled his way across the country to the Southwest, crossing the border into Mexico. After returning from Mexico to live in Arizona, he sent for his relatives and friends. "That," he said later, "was how the Syrian community began in Arizona." Similarly, in about 1882 a group of misrouted Arabs settled in Montreal, Quebec. The area proved a lucrative spot for peddlers, and soon they were joined by family and friends. This pattern was repeated with such regularity that a network of Syrian suppliers and their settlements soon stretched across North America, opening up opportunities for thousands of new arrivals.

To get their start in the trade, and for ongoing support and camaraderie, the immigrants turned to the peddling settlements, which reminded them of the villages they had left behind in Syria. In the settlements, peddlers returning from the road refreshed their spirits with laughter, drink, and song. They exchanged peddling stories, spoke with old friends in their native language, and enjoyed familiar food. The peddlers lived frugally in the settlements, crowded together in unlit, unheated, and unfurnished rooms. Most of them could have afforded better accommodations, but they preferred to save their money during what they intended to be a temporary stay in America.

The communities formed by the peddlers helped them adjust to life in America. Suppliers, who acted as leaders of their settlements, mediated disputes and provided advice and assistance to new arrivals and veterans alike. They also served as links to the outside world, receiving and forwarding peddlers' mail and banking their savings. And of course, suppliers provided recent immigrants with an almost immediate source of income, outfitting, orienting, and sending them out on the road very soon after their arrival.

When a new peddler arrived, the supplier provided basic instructions, explaining how to greet customers, exhibit goods, and request food and lodging. Suppliers also taught new immigrants the value of American currency and how to make a healthy profit. A few peddlers obtained their *kashshi*, the notions case central to their trade, from their supplier, but most generally purchased merchandise from him on credit. Within a day or two, they put their packs on their backs and set out to ply their trade in the nearby towns and countryside.

On the Road

For protection and companionship, peddlers usually traveled in pairs or in larger groups of relatives and friends. Some left the settlements for days or weeks at a time; the most ambitious might be on the road for months before returning. In the early days, peddlers traveled on foot, trudging over miles of dusty, muddy, or frozen country roads and carrying packs or suitcases that sometimes weighed more than 200 pounds. Later, horse-drawn rigs and automobiles enabled them to carry more merchandise and cover more territory.

Though American men often did not trust the Arab peddlers, isolated farm wives and housebound small-town homemakers awaited their arrival with great anticipation. Most Syrian peddlers sold practical wares, but to their customers their packs seemed an exciting bazaar of almost anything they might need or desire. Notions, ribbon, and lace; icons, trinkets, and jewelry; gingham, calico cloth, clothing, and more filled their cases. In addition to goods purchased from wholesalers in New York City, the peddlers often sold items that they or their families had made. They also brought news from their travels and excited the imaginations of their customers with "the wisdom of the East."

Syrian peddlers became a colorful fixture of life in America before World War I, and tales about them filled folklore and literature. In *The Laugh Peddler*, a book for children, Alice E. Christgau immortalized a "jolly, lovable peddler" who often came to her father's farm in Minnesota. The farmer in the story distrusts the peddler, but his wife and children eagerly look forward to the peddler's visits because they interrupt the monotony of farm life. Witty and wise, the peddler is courageous, as well. In one episode, for instance, when two of the farmer's children get lost in a blizzard, the peddler bravely rescues them. Similar stories abounded in real life.

The peddlers themselves preserved their experiences in scores of humorous anecdotes. When they returned to the settlements after weeks or months on the road, they shared stories of their adventures with their comrades. Beneath their humor, the tales reflect the pain, fatigue, and fear that accompanied peddlers on their travels. Faris N. wrote of a typical night on the road, when he had the responsibility of finding shelter for himself and a fellow villager's wife. After being turned away from several houses, he recalled the following story:

> I saw, on the side of the road, a small building. I jumped the fence . . . it had windows and a round door which was closed. I opened my kashshi and I used a scissors, No. 9, and I put it under the frame of the window and it opened and we entered. We saw two cases . . . I told her that this room had two beds, one for her and one for me. From our fatigue and the darkness, we did not see the graves . . . Then the moon came out. The woman cried out . . . "We are sleeping in a mausoleum and the dead are beneath us in the boxes." And she leaped out of the shed and I after her . . . we found a schoolhouse and we slept there until morning.

The peddlers' stories tell of rebuffs and insults; of scorching heat and parched throats; of long, hungry nights spent in cold barns or on wet grass; of frostbite and frozen skirts that slashed women's ankles; of being mired in mud, robbed, beaten, and lost; of fellow peddlers who were killed; of being chased by dogs and gun-toting farmers. "How do you tell a dog to go away if it

doesn't understand Arabic?" lamented one peddler.

The language barrier presented major problems for the peddlers. Although they tried to communicate through sign language and a few mispronounced words, most knew that English was a necessity. Without a basic command of the language, they might manage to ask questions but often could not understand the answers given. Wedad F. wrote of the time her aunt asked, "Boo, boo, boo, time?" at a train station and received the answer "Ten till two" from the stationmaster. When she missed the only train that passed through town that day, she asked her family, "Two? Two? Two, I understand, but what is this 'tentil'?" Faced with such problems, peddlers quickly learned English from their customers and from the farm families they lodged with.

Syrian women such as Wedad F.'s aunt thrived as peddlers, often having greater success than their male counterparts. Customers often trusted women peddlers more than men peddlers and tended to buy more from them and allow them easier access to their homes. Perhaps 75 to 80 percent of immigrant Syrian women peddled, making a significant economic contribution to the economy of the Syrian-American community. They endured the difficulties of life on the road in order to help their families achieve their goals.

Peddlers who acquired horse-and-buggy rigs could travel farther and bring a wider variety of goods to their customers. This peddler was based in Urbana, Illinois.

Despite the hardships of their trade, most Syrians felt neither discouraged nor depressed by their experiences. The immigrants concentrated instead on turning adversity into success. "We endured a lot," remembered Matt I., "but with all that I enjoyed this country because I was free and was making money." Relying on their wits, the Syrian peddlers persevered. They saved enough money to pay their debts, sent promised money orders back home, and paid the fare to America for their families.

Some successful peddlers used their earnings to expand their business. They started selling more expensive merchandise, such as imported rugs and linens. When they established a wealthy clientele, these peddlers' perceptions of themselves changed. They dressed fashionably and began to call themselves "salespeople." Selling status items proved highly lucrative, in addition to giving these Syrians prestige in the community. Many later used their profits and contacts to stop traveling and become suppliers or retail merchants.

During the peak peddling years before World War I, peddlers' annual income averaged $1,000. At that time, farm laborers, factory workers, and miners earned about $650 per year at best. Because peddling generated such substantial profits, the Syrians' expectations of how much they could earn were raised. They vigorously pursued the goal of making money, and while they did so, they made an invaluable contribution to American commerce. By distributing the products of small American industries throughout the country, the immigrants helped these industries grow, thereby fostering the economic health of the nation.

The era of peddling eventually drew to a close. By the time World War I broke out, the innovative American economy had outgrown the need for the peddlers' services. Mass production of consumer goods, the advent of department stores, and the success of mail-order catalogs made peddling obsolete. Few Syrians mourned its end; indeed, most had tired of the trade. The immigrants quickly adapted to the change, using peddling as a bridge to new enterprises. Instead of carrying their wares through the countryside, they established such retail businesses as dry goods stores and grocery stores. Others opened restaurants, poolrooms, movie houses, or confectionery shops. When they failed, which they did frequently, these entrepreneurs simply went on to try something else.

Muslim and Druze Syrians who immigrated at the end of the peddling era sometimes started their own family businesses, as well. Although Druze immigrants generally avoided factory work, most Muslims, joined by some Christian Arabs, went to work as laborers, lured by rising industrial wages. In 1914, for instance, the Ford Motor Company started paying the unprecedented wage of five dollars a day for eight hours of work. Syrians gravitated to industrial centers such as Toledo, Ohio; Michigan City, Indiana; and Highland Park, Michigan, to take advantage of the wartime boom in industry. In 1916, a large group of Muslim Arabs settled in Dearborn, Michigan, a suburb of Detroit near River Rouge, where Ford had recently moved its main plant. Today Dearborn boasts one of the largest and most visible Muslim communities in the United States.

Whether as laborers, peddlers, or merchants, Syrians prospered in America. But something unexpected happened while they pursued their dreams of wealth: They discovered the ideals of freedom, democracy, and equal opportunity and eagerly embraced American values as the country's true gold. Instead of working toward the day when they would return to their native land, they turned their attention to establishing communities and families and to becoming American. Because the Syrian peddlers' contact with customers had familiarized them with American ways, they adjusted to their new home more rapidly and easily than members of many other ethnic groups. ∽

Some Syrian immigrants, including women, chose jobs in industries such as automobile manufacturing.

*Most Syrian immigrants enjoyed
life in the New World and
enthusiastically expressed their
love for America.*

LIVING IN "AMRIKA"

In the late 19th and early 20th centuries, Syrian immigrants in the United States settled mostly in the Northeast and the Midwest, but peddling dispersed them all across the country, from New York to California and from Minnesota to Louisiana. Major cities such as New York, Chicago, and Boston supported thriving colonies, while lesser settlements sprang up in smaller towns built alongside railroad lines—Fort Wayne, Indiana; Cedar Rapids, Iowa; Spring Valley, Illinois; and Worcester, Massachusetts, for example.

The larger communities encompassed several neighborhoods, forming "Little Syrias." More typically, settlements consisted of a few Syrian-occupied houses sprinkled throughout the low-rent part of town. Working-class Americans or immigrants from other countries might live next door; Syrian children played with children of other nationalities; and often Christian Arabs attended church with their non-Arab neighbors. The few Muslims and Druze, who practiced their religion at home, went largely unnoticed by the American community. Syrians of the various religious sects characteristically lived separately, often in different neighborhoods, as they had done in their villages back home.

Immigrants clustered in peddling settlements, at first retaining their native customs.

Relatively few in number and scattered in small groups throughout the country, Syrians were spared much of the xenophobic sentiment that made life difficult for many other immigrant groups. For the most part, Americans did not feel economically threatened by Syrians, and Syrian religion, politics, and social behavior did not attract much attention from their neighbors. There were exceptions, of course. For instance, the police in Grand Rapids, Michigan, once arrested four Syrians when neighbors complained that the men were wearing "nightgowns" in public. Following Syrian custom, the immigrants had been relaxing on their front porch at day's end, smoking their *narghili* (water pipe) and sipping *araq* (a liqueur). The police released

(continued on page 57)

Slices of Arab-American life (clockwise): a family relaxes amid Old World furnishings in Cedar Rapids, Iowa; a metalworker draws a crowd in Fall River, Massachusetts; a customer admires a tapestry at Detroit's Arab World Festival; Arab Americans dance the debke *in Paramus, New Jersey.*

YEBRA GRAPE LEAF ROLLS ... 1.50
SFEEHA .... .50
KIBBY .... 2 for 1.00
HOMOS bi TAHINI ...... .75
HOT DOGS .... .40
HAMBURGERS .... .60
COFFEE .... .15
PASTRY
MAMOOL ..... 3 for 1.00
BAKLAWA .... .50
GRABEE .... .25

For many years now, Middle
Eastern specialties have added
spice to America's food, as
shown by these photos:
clockwise, a bakery display on
Atlantic Avenue in Brooklyn,
New York; a menu featuring
historically low prices at a
Detroit eatery; and a sumptuous
repast in Fall River,
Massachusetts.

Ties to the Middle East have remained strong in the American Midwest. This mosque (above) offers a spiritual home to Arab Americans in Detroit. Also in Detroit (above right), Arab Americans demonstrated for the Palestinian cause in the 1980s. At right, an Islamic Center in Cedar Rapids, Iowa, offers lessons in Arabic.

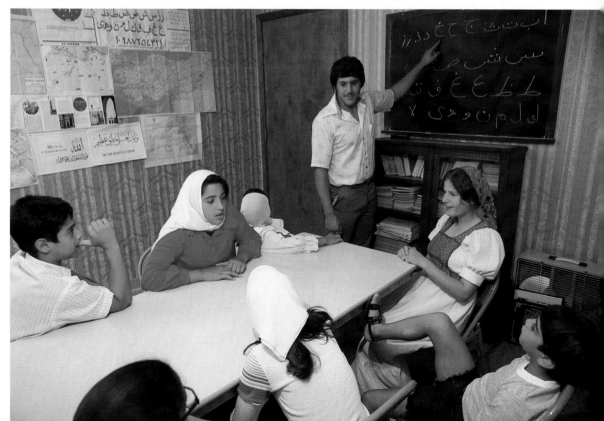

The Old World and the New receive equal tribute from this debke *troupe at Detroit's Arab World Festival.*

(continued from page 48)

them when their peddling supplier explained that they wore not nightgowns but a traditional Syrian costume, the *qumbaz*.

Within the Syrian settlements, 20 or more people frequently lived in a single house, and there was always room for one more new arrival. The peddlers crammed in 5, 10, or more to a room and usually lived without heat or electricity. After so much time spent on the road, they didn't require much other than room to lay their heads; as Tom A. wrote, "We didn't spend money for beds—we were here only temporarily." The crowded conditions allowed the immigrants to save money for the lives of ease they intended to live once they returned to Syria. In addition, the group houses reproduced village life and gave the peddlers a strong sense of community.

Each house had a communal kitchen that served as the center of the peddlers' social lives. There they shared meals and drank, played cards and told stories, and sang Arab songs. In the kitchen, peddlers returning from the road revived their spirits, and visitors enjoyed

In the 1890s, Dr. Ameen Haddad was a leader of the large Syrian colony in New York City, where many peddlers obtained their merchandise from wholesalers.

the Arab traditions of hospitality and generosity. As soon as they arrived, the peddlers gathered at the kitchen table to talk. Mayme F. recalled that they sometimes "liked to jump rope, wrestle, and barbecue lamb, and they had a wonderful time." When the immigrants arranged marriages, birthed babies, mourned deaths, and assisted each other in times of trouble, the kitchen was often the locus of activity.

In the American communities where they peddled, shopped, attended church, and relaxed in their free time, Syrian immigrants learned American ways. They picked up some English and observed unfamiliar customs such as Fourth of July and Thanksgiving Day celebrations. Raucous political torch parades, election-day roundups of voters to be taken to the polls, and workers' strikes seemed curious to people whose homeland had been occupied by an autocratic foreign government for four centuries. They saw or heard of important officials, such as senators, listening to the problems of citizens on the street. Even the president was called "mister," like any other man, and shook hands with ordinary people. The Syrians especially noticed the friendliness of the police. "I was never afraid of the police here. In the old country, the police are quick to hit you," observed Matt I.

Former peddlers often opened dry-goods stores with money saved during their time on the road and in settlements.

The Syrians frequently repeated the phrase "May God continue to bless this country," reflecting their fondness for America. The Arabic-language press also overflowed with praise for the United States. Syrian immigrants were beginning to settle in, and they yearned to establish homes and families. Married men sent for their wives and children; bachelors found brides among the single women in the peddling settlements or returned to their Syrian villages and brought their brides back with them.

Putting Down Roots

As peddling declined and more Syrian immigrants chose to remain in the United States, the number of families grew. Thus, the peddling colonies evolved into stable Arab-American communities. New York's Syrian colony, the first and largest in the New World, underwent this transition early on. In *Harper's Weekly*, W. Benough observed the colony on a Sunday in 1895:

> There is a queer mingling of American and Syrian costumes. Some of the prosperous young women are arrayed in all the glory of the latest picture-hats and most startling costumes of color, putting off the old and taking on the new with such vigor that there is no doubt at all about their American aspirations; others, less ambitious and less prosperous, still wear their picturesque lace or colored headdress.

Between 1890 and 1895 the New York community established some of the first churches for Arab-American Christians—one Maronite, one Melkite, and one Eastern Orthodox. By 1900 the colony supported three Arabic newspapers and several fraternal organizations, including a charitable society called the Daughters of Syria. Community leaders emerged from among the Syrian merchants and manufacturers. One of these, Dr. Ameen F. Haddad, was a graduate of the American University of Beirut. In 1892 he organized a Protestant

Born in the New World, the children of Syrian immigrants had to reconcile their parents' traditional values with their own American outlook.

Syrian Society, which operated a school to teach Syrian immigrants the English language, American citizenship, and other subjects.

By the time World War I broke out, shopkeeping had replaced peddling as the livelihood of most members of the Arab-American community. Syrians opened restaurants, hotels, ice cream parlors, poolrooms, butcher shops, and bakeries or worked as shoemakers, dry cleaners, jewelers, and tailors. A few Arabs operated banks, importing companies, publishing houses, manufacturing firms, or made a living as doctors, lawyers, dentists, realtors, farmers, and building contractors. But the overwhelming majority of Syrian entrepreneurs operated dry goods stores—offering many of the same items they had sold as peddlers—or grocery and fruit stores. Syrian-owned produce stores sprang up in towns across the country, and they monopolized the trade in a few cities during the 1920s.

Most Syrian stores started as family concerns located downstairs from or next door to the owner's home. The whole family helped out, allowing the store to stay open for long hours. In a 1975 issue of *Spectator* magazine, Raymond S. Azar described the Syrian-owned businesses of Terre Haute, Indiana, during the 1920s:

> Most of the groceries had residences attached, partly to hold down the cost of housing and partly to give the store owners a family life while working . . . up to 16 hours per day, 7 days a week. The attached residences also served to give the businessmen immediate stock, cashier, or meat counter help at the sound of a shout.

As soon as they were able, children helped make deliveries and stock the shelves. Instilled with family pride, individuals set aside their own desires to help the family achieve its material goals.

Wives managed their households and also helped their husbands in the business—canning preserves, waiting on customers, or cleaning. Sisters often left school or postponed marriage to help the family earn enough so that their brothers could attend college. Queenie N. married at the age of thirty-two. "I couldn't get married younger," she wrote, "because I had all those brothers to take care of. I worked to support my brothers." Sometimes women sacrificed even when their brothers' educations weren't at stake. "My family discouraged me from getting married because they wanted me to work," Nellie B. recalled. When her father died, her oldest brother inherited the business, and for fifty years she "never stopped working."

A few Syrian Americans entered the garment industry and met with the success dreamed of by all immigrant groups. They followed a tradition of textile manufacturing that had started in the New York colony before the turn of the century. Syrians there produced lace, linen, and other items, and Syrians in Los Angeles later started turning out bed linens, lingerie, and women's apparel. Two of the most successful Syrians in the industry were Mansour Farah and Joseph Marion Haggar. Unbeknownst to each other, both chose to settle in Texas to seek their fortunes.

Mansour Farah left Mt. Lebanon in 1905 and made his way to New Mexico via Canada. At the age of 20, he went into retailing with his brother and a few years later married, fathering two sons. In 1920, Farah went to New York City to learn about shirt design and manufacturing. Three months later he moved his family to El Paso, Texas, and opened a small factory that produced a single product: blue chambray work shirts. At first, Farah served as designer, cutter, salesperson, and janitor for his budding enterprise. The business prospered and expanded its line to include denim pants and bib overalls, though work shirts were dropped because prison factories turned them out more cheaply. Upon Farah's death in 1937, his two sons took control of the company. When they landed a contract during World War II to manufacture khaki clothing for the U.S. Army, they started the Farah Company on a course of expansion and diversification that continues today.

Three years after Farah came to this country, 17-year-old Joseph Marion Haggar arrived in the United States. He got his start in the garment business as a cotton grader and later was a sales agent for a dry goods company and a traveling peddler of overalls. During these years he worked in Texas, Louisiana, Missouri, and Oklahoma, and married and had two sons. In 1926 he moved to Dallas, Texas, bought a few sewing machines, hired four employees, and started his own business manufacturing work pants. Haggar's innovative assembly-line approach to making clothes became a model for the entire industry. He met with enormous success and eventually established the Haggar Company as the world's largest manufacturer of men's dress slacks.

Theodore Gantos also prospered in the apparel trade, though as a merchant rather than as a manufacturer. He immigrated to Canada in 1924 and later moved to Grand Rapids, Michigan, where he peddled linen and saved his money. He accumulated enough capital to open a small linen shop but went out of business when the stock market crashed in 1929. He returned to peddling and married his business partner, Haseebie Laham. In 1932 the couple opened another store together. Haseebie managed it while Theodore continued peddling to pay the bills. By 1937 the Gantoses had built a thriving business. Theodore quit peddling, and they moved their shop to the main business street of Grand Rapids. That shop was only the first in a nationwide chain of women's clothing stores operated by Gantos's sons since his death in 1970.

After making a fortune in the clothing industry, Joseph Haggar donated millions of dollars to charity.

Syrian-American women made tremendous economic contributions to their families and, as wage earners, gained some freedom from Old World restrictions.

For immigrants such as Gantos, Haggar, and Farah, hard work led to prosperity. Few other Syrians enjoyed such tremendous success, but many soon joined the ranks of the American middle class and bought homes in better neighborhoods. Merchants often used their profits to expand their businesses, which they then passed on to their children. Some children gladly continued the family tradition, although they modernized the businesses and put a distinctly American stamp on them. But some of the younger American-born, college-educated children left their fathers' businesses behind to pursue more prestigious "American" careers.

The assimilation process gained momentum during and after World War I. Many young Syrian men broadened their horizons while serving in the armed forces. After 1924, with the institution of immigration quotas, there were fewer new arrivals to remind the Syrians of their homeland. As Arabs adopted the social attitudes, manners, and accents of New England, the South, and the Midwest, Arab-American communities blended into the regional cultures surrounding them. Syrians increasingly Americanized their names to avoid the difficulties of pronouncing and spelling Arabic sounds not found in English. Many acquired citizenship.

Family Ties

Although Syrians sought acceptance as Americans, they did not shed all their own values and traditions. They especially continued to cherish family honor and unity. As they had in their homeland, Syrian Americans expected family members to defend and enhance the family's honor and status and to conform their will and interests to those of the family. In return for loyalty, the family conferred prestige upon its members and provided protection and a sense of identity. Syrian values centered on pride in one's family name and ancestry, dedication to the family's religious beliefs, respect for elders, and loyalty to parents in their old age. In matters relating to people outside the family, Arabs prized generosity, hospitality, learning, and individualism—much as they had done in Syria.

The paramount importance of the family and the tendency of Arabs to define themselves according to family name, religious sect, and village of origin sometimes bred clannishness and factionalism within the Arab-American community. But the obligation to protect and enhance family honor and status produced a competitive spirit that in turn bred an ethic of hard work, thrift, perseverance, shrewdness, and conservatism. The fear of bringing shame and dishonor to the family name seemed to discourage most Arab Americans from committing crimes or accepting financial assistance from the government. Few Arab names showed up on criminal-court dockets or relief rolls, even during the Great Depression of the 1930s.

Despite the Syrians' adherence to traditional values, Americanization had a profound effect on their family life. In the Arab world, the oldest male member of each family headed an extended group that generally included several generations. As Syrians adopted American conventions, nuclear families replaced large patriarchal families. The influence of patriarchs on the daily lives of family members gradually diminished, although the respect they commanded as family heads did not. Syrian family strength and solidarity remained the rule.

Growing numbers of married sons chose to head their own households instead of bringing their wives to live with them in their fathers' homes. Single men, influenced by their American educations, increasingly left home to pursue economic opportunity or other interests. Conditions for unmarried women, who had traditionally stayed within the extended patriarchal family until their parents selected husbands for them, also changed. In the New World more and more women exercised the right to marry men of their own choosing. Whomever they married, they started families of their own with their new husbands.

As soldiers in World War I, Syrian-American men asserted their loyalty to the United States and broadened their knowledge of the world.

Syrian-American women contributed to the war effort as nurses and industrial workers.

The role of women in the Syrian family and community evolved slowly. Peddling and shopkeeping required husbands to spend a great deal of time outside the home, so women assumed greater authority within the family. Although they kept their customary roles as wives, mothers, and housekeepers, many women also peddled or worked in family businesses. Their greater authority within the home and the incomes they earned outside it enhanced some women's positions and gave them more independence. For most, however, limited access to education and indoctrination into the notions of obedience, sacrifice, chastity, and male superiority continued to restrict their autonomy.

By the 1920s, the children of the early Syrian immigrants had become more American than Syrian.

Christian Syrians adjusted fairly readily to shifting social currents. By World War II, Christian women mixed with men at public and church gatherings. Many Christian wives and mothers responded to new demands on their time by having fewer children and cooking fewer Arabic dishes, which took long hours to prepare. Change, however, did not come as quickly to the Muslim and Druze communities. Conservative Islamic family values supported patriarchal authority and helped restrict women to traditional roles. Muslim and particularly Druze men took the first step toward change when some of them, usually motivated by the simple shortage of women of their faith in America, married Christians. Still, interfaith marriages among Arabs remained unusual until after World War II.

Second-generation Arab Americans, especially those who grew up in the 1920s, were soon swept along by a tide of liberalization. Automobiles, radio, movies, and electrical appliances altered the fabric of American life, and along with it the lives of Arab Americans. Bobbed hair and higher hemlines shocked the nation and signaled the loosening of social restrictions. American women started working in factories and won the right to vote, and Syrian-American women cautiously but inexorably freed themselves from restrictive traditions. A few even chose husbands from outside the Syrian community.

In addition, many Syrian-American men who had served in the U.S. military during World War I had acquired a heightened sense of American patriotism. They had lived, worked, and socialized with other young men from across the country and had learned about the world outside their parents' communities. More than ever, they wanted to become American and in response to this desire some married non-Syrian women. During the 1920s the number of Syrian Americans marrying those from other ethnic groups increased dramatically. At the same time, fewer and fewer children born to Syrian families had immigrant parents. Faced with the rapid erosion of its ethnic identity, the Syrian-American community rushed to establish churches and fraternal organizations to preserve Syrian customs. ❧

*Christian Syrian immigrants
brought their Eastern-rite
religious traditions with them
to North America.*

TRADITION AND ASSIMILATION

T he growth of Syrian-American religious, social, and journalistic institutions heralded the transformation of settlements and colonies into permanent communities. Though generally established to help preserve Syrian ethnic identity in the New World, many of these institutions contributed to the assimilation process started while peddling, by making life in North America more satisfying for the immigrants. Once they could attend churches, join clubs, and read newspapers of their own, Syrians felt truly settled in their new home.

Arab-American institutions developed at different times throughout America. Larger populations established churches, fraternal alliances, and newspapers fairly early on and smaller communities a little later, but in many areas of the country Syrian colonies remained too small or factionalized to support any formal institutions at all. Even within the smallest settlements Syrians rarely crossed religious or village lines to set up nonsectarian organizations. Social clubs and fraternal benefit societies for Syrians of different religious backgrounds often predated churches wherever Syrians of the same faith were too few in number to build a place of worship.

Bishop Raphail Hawaweeny, ordained in 1904, built the first Syrian Orthodox cathedral in the United States.

Transplanting the Faith

Churches and mosques represented the most powerful force for the survival of Syrian culture. They allowed members of the same faith to gather, share familiar rituals, reinforce their common bonds and beliefs, and communicate their values to their children. Many religious groups prayed in homes or rented halls until they could build churches of their own. Some of them depended on infrequent visits by priests, or *imams* (Muslim religious teachers), who traveled from community to community. Itinerant clergy conducted services in Arabic and performed religious rites such as marriages, baptisms, and funerals. Between their visits, however, lay long stretches of time during which the immigrants frequently sought spiritual sustenance elsewhere.

Many Syrians simply joined American churches. Maronites and Melkites often chose the Roman Catholic church, whereas followers of the Eastern Orthodox church gravitated toward Episcopalianism. Syrian clergy in the New World and back home feared that the immigrants would stray from Eastern-rite beliefs. But because these sects had too few members and resources in America to build churches for many years, they lost numerous members to established American churches.

Hoping to keep their communities intact, Arab-American women took the lead in building churches and mosques. In America, women had gained some new social and economic freedoms, and they put them to use serving their communities. When they saw a need to build a church or mosque, they established clubs to organize fund-raising events. They tried to recruit the often reluctant men to help on their projects, but even when men did not get involved women continued to pursue their objective. A man in one Syrian community noted that "if it weren't for them, we wouldn't have a church." Between 1895 and 1940, Syrian Christians built a total of about 115 churches in the United States. Women's success in raising funds, and their pivotal role in establishing Syrian parishes, enhanced their power and status in their respective communities.

Muslims, who had arrived later and in smaller numbers than Christians, set up only four mosques before World War II. They were hampered by the fact that Muslim women did not come to North America until the 1920s. Without women, Muslim families, communities, and institutions had little chance to develop. In addition, living and working in a Christian society forced Muslims to make significant adjustments to the way in which they practiced their religion. Most could no longer pray facing Mecca five times a day, observe the Sabbath on Friday, or fast during the Muslim holy month, Ramadan. They made up for this, however, by meeting their religious obligations in other ways allowed for in Islamic Holy Law. They could, for example, compensate for missed prayers by contributing extra money to charity or to the religious education of young Muslims.

Hobbled by Druze policy forbidding religious leaders to be trained in foreign lands or to emigrate from the homeland, Druze immigrants did not build a place of worship in America until 1990. However, few Druze immigrants felt bound to a rigid interpretation of their esoteric faith. Because they believed in the same God as that worshiped by Christians and Jews, most felt comfortable attending Christian churches.

As Syrians assimilated and fewer of their American-born children and grandchildren learned to speak Arabic, growing numbers of Arab Americans stayed away

Before World War II, Muslim immigrants established only four mosques, including this one in Cedar Rapids, Iowa.

73

Syrian-American women formed numerous social and civic organizations, some dedicated to building churches.

from church. To encourage their members to attend, Syrian churches gradually Americanized their liturgies. The clergy participated more actively in community life and developed church-sponsored social and educational programs to attract the descendants of the immigrants. The distinction between Syrian and American churches blurred, but loyalty to the Syrian churches was strengthened.

Community Bonds

Syrian Americans formed fraternal organizations to meet the social needs of the group. These societies often arose out of the impromptu meetings held by peddlers to discuss early settlement concerns such as how to help the needy or bury the dead. In many settlements, the informal meetings evolved into societies that elected officers and held formal votes on issues of importance to the group.

As increasing numbers of Syrians established themselves in the United States, they created many types of organizations to serve educational, charitable, and social functions. Syrian Americans set up English language and American citizenship classes, groups that helped Syrian immigrants become American citizens, and societies that fostered understanding between Syrians and other Americans. Some societies formed around family name, village of origin, or religious sect and raised funds to build schools, orphanages, churches, and hospitals in Syria.

In addition to addressing the wider needs of the Syrian community, meetings of these organizations gave members the chance to socialize with old friends and to make new ones. In order to strengthen loyalty to the religious sect and ensure its continuity, the leaders of these societies encouraged the formation of groups where young Arab Americans could meet and perhaps form relationships that would lead to marriage. The American-born children of these organization members, however, had their own ideas about their future in the United States.

Some young Arab Americans got involved in American in addition to Syrian organizations. George Addes, for instance, joined the labor movement of the 1930s and fought alongside Walter Reuther, a longtime union activist from West Virginia, to organize automobile workers in Detroit. Addes hoped to improve conditions for all automobile workers, but particularly for the many Syrian immigrants who had flocked to Michigan to find work in the industry. Addes and his colleagues fought long and hard to win recognition for the United Automobile Workers (UAW). In 1941 they succeeded

Many Syrian-American social clubs attracted large memberships and sponsored lavish banquets and other events.

in completely unionizing the automobile industry, and Addes became the first secretary-treasurer of the UAW.

In the 1920s, the immigrants' children began to found their own organizations, as well. They rejected their parents' highly traditional orientation and formed Americanized clubs. Much to the dismay of older Syrians, these second-generation organizations deemphasized old-world traditions and discouraged the Syrian tendency toward clannishness. Many opened their membership to Syrian Americans of all religions and villages of origin.

Salloum Mokarzel, an Americanized Syrian immigrant, hoped to mediate between the younger and older generations and to alleviate the factionalism among fraternal societies. The younger brother of a New York publisher, Mokarzel had published a monthly English-language journal, *The Syrian World*, since 1926. In it, he began to call for the formation of a league of social clubs.

During the short life of *The Syrian World*, Mokarzel tried but failed to unite America's Syrian clubs into a single federation. The unification movement he encouraged did have some success in 1932, however, when Syrians in Boston formed a federation of local organizations throughout the eastern United States. In this federation, clubs "of any faith or purpose" joined to sponsor social activities and to build a bridge between Syrian Americans and the American community. Other regional federations also developed, but Arab-American clubs had no national organization until the 1950s.

The Press

The Syrian World was but one of many Arab American publications. The Arabic press at once perpetuated Syrian ethnicity and encouraged the assimilation of Syrian immigrants into American life. From its earliest days until the end of World War II the New York colony, the home of a small Syrian intellectual community, was the center of activity for Syrian journalists. The first

Arabic newspaper published in the New World, *Kawkab Amrika* (*The Star of America*), made its debut in 1892. Started by two brothers, Najib and Ibrahim Arbeely, the paper began as a weekly and later became a daily. *Kawkab Amrika* brought the Syrian community local news and news from the homeland and published Syrian folklore until its presses closed down in 1907.

By that time, Syrian-American readers had a number of other newspapers to choose from. An estimated 50 Arabic newspapers circulated in the United States by 1930, but they competed so fiercely that many lasted only a few months. Three that survived stayed in business for more than 60 years. *Al-Hoda* (*The Guidance*), founded by Salloum Mokarzel's brother Naoum in 1898, served the Maronite community and had the widest influence of any Syrian paper. *Mirat al-Gharb* (*Mirror of the West*) started publishing in 1899 and addressed Eastern Orthodox readers, and the leading Muslim and Druze paper, *al-Bayan* (*The Explanation*) printed its first issue in 1911.

The Arabic newspapers informed immigrant readers about events in their homeland, reported on Syrian activity in America, and printed immigrant success stories. Their editorials and feature stories introduced Syrian immigrants to social, economic, and political life in America. Though they tended to idealize and oversimplify the character of life in America, these articles eased the Syrians' adjustment to their new home. Most of the editorials urged readers to give up traditional ways that might interfere with their success in the New World.

At the same time, however, the Arabic press proved instrumental in preserving the Syrian heritage in America. The papers nurtured contemporary Arab culture by printing the works of immigrant writers and poets, and Syrian-American newspaper publishers in New York frequently distributed Arabic books published both in the homeland and in America. For the first time, villagers who had had little access to newspapers and libraries in the old country could read about the

As secretary-treasurer of the United Automobile Workers, George Addes helped increase industrial production during World War II.

Arabic newspapers such as Kawkab Amrika *often served as forums for discussions about the Americanization of Syrian immigrants.*

society, politics, history, and literature of their own land—and that of the rest of the world.

A small group of writers and poets who called themselves the Pen League composed many of the literary works published in the Arabic press. Led by Kahlil Gibran, an internationally renowned author, the Pen League was formed around 1913 to foster the Arabic literary movement in America. Pen League writers worked from the centuries-old Arabic poetic tradition, which a group of Syrian poets at the American University in Beirut had adapted to English speech and the tonal quality of Protestant hymns. In the United States, Arabic writers started a revolution in Arabic literature, influenced by the informal "free verse" of such poets as Walt Whitman. Pen League members published their works in the Arabic newspapers and also in their own literary journal. But because literacy in Arabic was declining, they found only a small audience, and the Pen League was dissolved in 1931.

The leader of the Pen League had much greater success than the organization he helped found. Born in 1883, Kahlil Gibran arrived in New York City in 1912. A champion of Americanization, Gibran wrote an article for an Arabic newspaper in Boston in 1919 exhorting "the children of the first generation Arabs to proudly preserve their heritage in their quest for citizenship." He later published a message "To Young Americans of Syrian origin" in the periodical *Syrian World*, urging his readers to "be proud of being an American, but . . . also to be proud that your fathers and mothers came from a land upon which God laid His gracious hand and raised His messengers."

In addition to essays, Gibran wrote poetry and novels in both English and Arabic and gained some recognition as a visual artist as well. In 1923 he published *The Prophet*, his most famous work, in English. The volume has since been translated into at least 20 other languages, and the American edition alone has sold more than 9 million copies. Filled with deeply religious and mystical symbolism, the verse contained in *The Prophet* reflects the influence of the poet William Blake and the philosopher Friedrich Nietzsche on Gibran's style. The book also reveals an Arab philosophy of life, as in the following passage:

And what is it to work with love?
It is to weave the cloth with threads drawn from your heart, even as if your beloved were to wear that cloth.
It is to build a house with affection, even as if your beloved were to dwell in that house.
It is to sow seeds with tenderness and reap the harvest with joy, even as if your beloved were to eat the fruit.

It is to charge all the things you fashion with the breath of your own spirit,
And to know that all the blessed dead are standing about you and watching.

Whereas Gibran's work enjoyed tremendous popularity, many newspapers that published in Arabic went out of business during the years between the two world wars because the number of Arab Americans who still read the language declined precipitously. The children and grandchildren of Americanized Syrians showed little interest in learning the Arabic language, and the 1924 immigration quota act that brought a virtual halt to Syrian immigration to the United States dealt another crippling blow to Arabic publishers. It deprived them of their largest group of readers—new arrivals.

Because it signaled the fading vitality of Syrian culture in the New World, the declining use of Arabic worried Salloum Mokarzel. In *The Syrian World*, he championed Americanization and criticized many Syrian traditions, yet at the same time he attempted to preserve Syrian culture and transmit it to the younger generation. Mokarzel knew that Syrians born and raised in America knew little about their ethnic history, language, and heritage. He published *The Syrian World* to "breed in them a consciousness of appreciation for their racial qualities and inheritances so that they may comport themselves with a befitting sense of honor as citizens of this great American nation." He and other leading Arabic writers used the English-language journal to urge Syrian Americans to remember and appreciate their heritage while pursuing their new American interests. Imitating American publications, Mokarzel invited readers to discuss the issue of assimilation in letters to the journal.

By 1932, when the Great Depression forced *The Syrian World* to fold, the journal had achieved a reputation and circulation that no Arabic publication has since equaled. The number and quality of Arabic journals

Kahlil Gibran, a leader of the Syrian-American community, wrote The Prophet, *a book of poetry reflecting his Arab origins.*

shrank steadily until the 1950s, when the press enjoyed a brief revival. The early immigrant generations had given rise to a vital Syrian press, but the Americanization of later generations transformed it into a collection of small local publications of lesser editorial quality.

In some respects, the Arabic press and the Pen League were exceptions to a tradition that placed material success before intellectual and artistic pursuit. Most early immigrants came to the New World in order to make money, and they succeeded through hard work and good luck, not through book learning. Only a few educated Arabs made their way to the New York colony

Unlike many children of work-oriented Syrian immigrants, Dr. Rosa Lee Nemir had the support of her family while she pursued a medical education.

or to various American universities to join the intellectual community. Philip K. Hitti, one such immigrant, arrived in the United States in 1913 to complete the education he had started in Syria. In 1915 he received a Ph.D. in history and started his career as a professor. During his long tenure at Princeton University, Hitti earned a reputation as a leading authority on the Middle East.

More American than Syrian

If, like Hitti, second-generation Syrian Americans wanted to pursue careers outside the world of business, they sometimes had to overcome the resistance of their families. John Kacere, who became a successful artist, came from a working-class community that did not understand his ambitions. Early in his life, he realized that "the Lebanese people, generally speaking, are not culturally inclined." Born to immigrant parents who ran a grocery store in Walker, Iowa, he later recalled that "as a child, I would feel left out." Kacere left home at 18 to study art in Chicago. He went on to receive international recognition in his field but still found that the older members of the Syrian community did not "think I was working because I didn't go to work at eight to five every day. . . . They wouldn't take my work seriously, even if I earned $500 a day to their $400 a week."

Nonetheless, second-generation Syrian Americans often sought college educations at American universities, and some went on to careers in science, public service, or education. Rosa Lee Nemir had the support of her family when she decided to take advantage of the opportunities unavailable to women in Syria. When she graduated from her Austin, Texas, high school in 1922, she went on to college, and from there to the Johns Hopkins Medical School in Baltimore, Maryland. After completing her training in San Francisco and New York in 1932, Dr. Nemir embarked on a lifetime of medical practice, research, and teaching. The medical community honored her with numerous awards for her contributions to the study of children's lung disease and to the advancement of women in medicine.

Education allowed Syrian Americans to assimilate, but in their eagerness to integrate into the prospering American society, early Syrian immigrants and their children neglected to preserve their own culture. Syrians assimilated so rapidly that the second generation of Syrian Americans seemed more American than Syrian. Although this situation worried some older Syrians, they found themselves powerless to prevent or even slow down the process. Syrian assimilation into American culture accelerated between the two world wars. Young Syrian Americans seldom knew more about their ancestral culture than that it had produced the traditional food, music, and dances they enjoyed in their parents' homes on special family days and religious holidays.

Wedad F., who immigrated in 1921 at the age of six, reflects on the assimilation of Syrian youth:

> I've heard my parents say that Syria was the seat of all learning and culture. They always beat that drum but us kids didn't know what that meant. . . . So, what is Syrian culture? . . . I don't know . . . I suppose it was to be hospitable in your home, serve tons of food, speak the [Arabic] language, respect your elders—well, you know, marry someone of your own religion. Oh, yes, protect that family name! Maybe the old people talked about it, but not us. To tell you the truth, I don't know anyone of my generation who cared much.

The children of American-born Syrians found they could learn little about their heritage from their parents. Syrian Americans might have Americanized themselves beyond recognition if a second wave of Arabic-speaking people had not migrated to the United States after World War II. Indeed, the new Arab immigrants soon discovered that they had little in common with first-wave immigrants and their descendants in the United States. ❧

*Arab immigrants arriving after
World War II felt a strong sense
of Arab national pride.*

THE NEW IMMIGRANTS

The Arab immigrants who have arrived in the New World since World War II differ in many important ways from those who came earlier, but they share some of the same motivations. They, too, come intending to stay only temporarily and for the purpose of improving their economic lot, and they, too, become permanent residents. Beyond that, however, the similarities end. Unlike earlier Syrian immigrants who worked as farmers and artisans in their homeland, most of the new arrivals have college degrees or seek to earn them in America. And in contrast to their Christian Syrian predecessors, most recent Arab immigrants are Muslims.

Thousands have fled the political turmoil that has plagued the Middle East since the formation of Israel in 1948, and emigration from the region accelerated markedly following the defeat of Egypt, Syria, and Jordan by Israel in the Six-Day War of 1967. The U.S. Immigration and Naturalization Service records indicate over 300,000 Arab arrivals since the end of World War II, but this figure does not count Arabs who enter the United States from Canada, South and Central America, or Europe after several years of residence there. Among the first to leave were Palestinian farmers who lost their land to Israel. Palestinians continue to arrive today and constitute the largest group of post–World War II Arab immigrants.

Postwar Arab immigrants frequently fled politically troubled homelands such as Lebanon.

Citizens of the rest of the Arab world, weary of constant fighting and economic problems in the region or hoping for better educational and career opportunities, have joined the Palestinians in the emigration. The decades since World War II have brought wealthy Egyptians, stripped of their property by government nationalization of businesses; poor peasants from southern Lebanon, displaced by Israeli invasions and the long and bloody civil war; Yemeni, Iraqi, and North African people seeking a better life; and many other Arabs in search of economic opportunity and political stability. Few, however, have left the relatively peaceful, religiously conservative, and increasingly prosperous oil-exporting countries of the Arabian Peninsula.

Unlike the earlier immigrants, who as subjects of the Ottoman Empire had never ruled themselves, the second wave of Arab immigrants originated in a group of independent states and carried with it a new Arab political consciousness. In 1945, 7 Arab states signed a pact forming the Arab League, which 14 other Middle-Eastern nations and the Palestinian Liberation Organization (PLO) later joined. The league encouraged its members and the rest of the world to recognize the culture and interests shared by all Arabs without regard to the artificial state boundaries imposed on the region by European powers.

The Arab League seeks to unite the Arabic-speaking peoples of the Middle East in the pursuit of common economic and political goals. The League has suffered many internal disputes (including a split over the 1991 Persian Gulf War, when nine members sent troops to support the anti-Iraq coalition), but it has strengthened Arab identity and pride. No matter what their country of origin, recent Arab immigrants have brought with them a nationalism that transcends the borders of their home countries. These new arrivals have revitalized Arab-American culture and revived the ethnic feelings of assimilated Syrian Americans.

Better Prospects

Immigrants traveling to the United States after World War II landed in a country that had grown into the world's leading industrial, scientific, and military power. Many of them thrived in their new surroundings because they came equipped with valuable professional skills and had the ability to speak English. They prospered at work and adjusted easily to life in America. A smaller group of working-class immigrants with little

Long-established Syrian-American communities attracted many second-wave Arab arrivals.

Working-class Arabs often settled in the Arab neighborhoods of Dearborn, Michigan, and went to work in automobile factories.

or no education made its way to established Arab communities and took jobs in industry or with Arab businesses. Whether educated or uneducated, the new immigrants hoped to make enough money in the United States to return home and live a comfortable life. Despite their original intentions, most stayed in America.

The improvement in the educational levels of post–World War II Arab immigrants had its roots in European rule of the Middle East after World War I. Western influence between the two world wars caused many wealthy Arab families to send their children to local and European universities. Arabs continued to attend foreign universities when they gained their independence after World War II.

Fledgling Arab governments instituted ambitious economic development programs intended to remedy the stagnation that had set in in the Middle East under colonial rule. As participants in this effort, thousands of young people went abroad, especially to the United States, for technical, financial, managerial, and social training. Unfortunately, internal disorder and the ongoing Arab-Israeli conflict interfered at home, and modernization there did not keep pace with education abroad. Faced with scant employment opportunities in their native countries, many highly educated young Arabs decided not to return. Others tried to make a go of it at home but grew frustrated with the lack of appropriate jobs and did not stay.

Many Arabs skirted U.S. immigration restrictions by entering the country on student visas and staying to work when they completed their education. Later, the professional-preference clause in the Immigration and Nationality Act of 1965 allowed many Arab professionals to immigrate legally. The emigration of educated people from the Middle East constituted a severe "brain drain" that peaked between 1968 and 1971. These immigrants could not resist the pull of opportunity. Whereas they had struggled to find work in their homelands, they had little difficulty obtaining jobs in their chosen fields in America. Upward mobility has char-

acterized their experience in the United States, and many
have become thoroughly Americanized.

White-collar immigrants settled wherever they found
jobs and established some new Arab communities in urban areas, such as the Egyptian Coptic (Christian) settlement in Los Angeles. Unskilled workers gravitated toward established Arab-American communities, where
they felt at home among the descendants of earlier Syrian
immigrants. One of the working-class immigrants' favored destinations was Dearborn, Michigan, a suburb of
Detroit that ranks among the largest Muslim communities in the United States. After the 1967 war several
thousand Muslim Palestinians, Yemenis, and southern
Lebanese, in addition to many well-educated immigrants, arrived there.

Until 1967 assimilated Syrian Americans and more
recent Arab immigrants lived as virtual strangers, having
little in common. The Arab defeat in the Six-Day War
and the resultant influx of Arab immigrants to the United
States changed all that. Many Americanized Syrians, dis-
tressed by the war's outcome and the rise of what they
perceived as anti-Arab bias, were introduced to Arab nationalism by the new immigrants and adopted their political outlook.

Because of the influx of so many new arrivals, Dearborn today resembles a "Little Syria" perhaps more
closely than any other contemporary Arab-American
community. In 1992, for example, an American Arab
Chamber of Commerce was organized by two Arab-
American businessmen, Ned Fawaz and Abraham Osta,
both of whom were immigrants to the United States. In
addition to publishing a newsletter and a business direc-
tory, the chamber offers its members services such as
health insurance, payroll processing, and seminars on
Middle East trade. The ambassadors from ten Arab
countries attended the chamber's annual banquet in
1996. Such community organizations can ease the adjustment of immigrants to their new home. They also
help forge a bond between newer Arab arrivals and descendants of the earlier Syrian immigrants.

*Unlike their Syrian
predecessors, most new
immigrants from the Arab
world practiced Islam.*

The continuing influx of Arabs to the United States helped Arab-American communities maintain their ethnic flavor.

The Ethnic Revival

The humiliating Arab defeat in 1967 instilled most Arab Americans with a sense of Arab nationalism and ethnic identity. They came to realize how strongly U.S. foreign policy favored Israel and watched as Arabs suffered ridicule and condemnation in the American media and in Congress. In the face of anti-Arab sentiment, the division between the descendants of the early Syrian immigrants and the new Arab immigrants faded. New immigrants and Americanized Syrians alike proudly referred to themselves as Arabs and took steps to preserve their language, ethnic identity, and heritage.

As the ethnic consciousness of Arab Americans increased, so did the vitality of various Arab-American institutions. The Arabic-language press, in serious decline before World War II, came back to life in the 1950s and found new purpose as the Arab-Israeli conflict intensified. Numerous Arabic and Arabic-English newspapers and journals appeared, although competition for a limited readership resulted in a short life span for most of the periodicals. The papers printed some social and cultural news but devoted most of their space to the politics and economics of the Middle East. As vehicles for the political opinions of their publishers, however, none of the newer publications achieved the editorial quality or national audience of earlier Arab papers.

The newly arrived Arab Americans founded clubs and associations of their own as the organizations started by earlier Syrian immigrants underwent some changes. Religious, family, and village societies arose to serve the recent immigrants. The educated, nationalistic Arabs set up cultural groups based on their nation of origin, and professional associations previously unfamiliar to Syrian Americans. At the same time, under the leadership of later generations of Syrian Americans, some of the older Syrian organizations formed regional and national federations and attempted to influence American opinion and policy regarding the Arab world. When Israel won the Six-Day War most of the diverse groups found they shared at least one concern: the political situation in the Middle East and its consequences for Arab Americans.

From the late 1960s through the 1980s, four national organizations were formed to influence U.S. policy in the Middle East and improve the image of Arabs in the United States. The Association of Arab American University Graduates, established in 1967, is composed mostly of academics and other professionals. The National Association of Arab Americans, founded in 1972, is the major Arab-American political lobby. The American-Arab Anti-Discrimination Committee, founded in 1980, soon became the largest Arab-American organization. In 1985, the Arab-American Institute was established to assist Arab Americans in seeking political office. These organizations remain active today. Besides using traditional media, they have begun sponsoring sites on the World Wide Web, and they have been joined in

Assimilated Syrian Americans soon shared the concern felt by second-wave immigrants regarding events in the Middle East.

this electronic outreach by newer organizations such as CaféArabica.

Since World War II, and especially since 1967, Arab-American religious institutions have taken a more active role in community affairs. The arrival of numerous Muslims in the United States spurred the establishment of many mosques throughout the country. It also revived Arab interest in learning Arabic because Arabic is an integral part of the practice of Islam. Immigrant imams taught and continue to teach it to their congregations along with modern Islamic thought. Sectarian activity gave Arab-American Muslims a stronger sense of community, and in an effort to achieve the same effect among Christians, the Arab churches began sponsoring community events and offering classes in language, history, and culture.

The effects of the new immigration and the Six-Day War complemented the growing American fascination with ethnicity in the 1960s and 1970s. Descendants of first-wave Syrian immigrants sought to revive their culture at the same time that the new immigrants worked to retain theirs. Some third- and fourth-generation Syrian Americans turned for an understanding of their heritage to their parents, who, unfortunately, could offer

Postwar Arab immigrants inspired new interest in the cultural heritage of the Arab world.

only vague, fragmentary information, much of it inaccurate. Arab-American college students had better luck when they joined Arab clubs or took courses in Arabic language and history.

This ethnic revival did not prevent the Americanization of the new immigrants' children. Whereas the children of Syrian Americans searched for their Arab roots, the children of the second-wave Arab immigrants attended American schools, watched American television and movies, and sought acceptance by their American friends. Like their counterparts in the 1920s, these new Arab Americans assimilated rapidly. Today Arab immigrants and their descendants are thoroughly American and have attained positions of prominence in almost every profession. Yet no matter how integrated they have become, most retain a sense of Arab identity born of a sharp awareness of the ongoing Arab-Israeli conflict and what it means for Arabs throughout the world. ∽

Many descendants of the early Syrian immigrants, such as Selwa Roosevelt, former U.S. chief of protocol, have enjoyed professional success yet have remained acutely aware of the ongoing Arab-Israeli conflict.

*Ralph Nader champions
environmental and
consumer protection
causes.*

MEETING THE CHALLENGE

Syrians came to the United States seeking opportunity and found it in abundance. As early as 1900, scores of Syrian immigrants had met success in trade and set the stage for their children's future prosperity. More recently, as assimilation and education have broadened their horizons, Arab immigrants and their descendants have entered the professions. Many have achieved prominence in such diverse fields as government, journalism, education, sports, and entertainment.

Americans of Arab descent have been particularly active in public service, the arena that produced perhaps the most famous Arab American: Ralph Nader. Born on February 27, 1934, Nader grew up in a small Connecticut town where his parents, Syrian immigrants, operated a restaurant and bakery. During dinnertime discussions, the Naders taught their four children about democracy and civic duty, thus inspiring their son Ralph to become a lawyer.

In 1951, Nader graduated from the Woodrow Wilson School of Public and International Affairs at Princeton University. He attended Harvard Law School and entered the army after his graduation in 1958. Later, as a lawyer in private practice and a journalist for the *Atlantic Monthly* and the *Christian Science Monitor*, Nader grew increasingly disturbed by the greed

In the latter part of his career, diplomat Philip Habib (right) dedicated himself to bringing peace to the Middle East.

and irresponsibility of American corporations, particularly those in the automobile industry. In 1964 he joined then-Assistant Secretary of Labor Daniel Patrick Moynihan to study highway safety.

Nader's work resulted in the publication in 1965 of *Unsafe at Any Speed*, his book condemning Detroit's disregard for safety in auto design. The exposé led to the passage of the Traffic and Motor Vehicle Safety Act in 1966, which made seat belts a mandatory feature in all new cars. Nader catapulted to fame, and he used his new clout to pursue other safety and consumer-protection issues. During the 1970s he formed a number of consumer advocacy groups, and the young lawyers he hired earned the nickname "Nader's Raiders" as they worked to disclose industrial and consumer hazards and instances of ineffective government.

Nader played an instrumental role in the creation of the Environmental Protection Agency, the Occupational Safety and Health Administration, and the Consumer Product Safety Commission. He was also a key figure in the passage of the Freedom of Information Act. In recent years, his organizations have addressed issues such as telecommunications and privacy. In 1996, he buoyed the environmental movement by running for president on the Green Party ticket. In one interview, he characterized the motivation behind his career as "a thirst for justice."

Another Arab American also had a tremendous impact on the world of public affairs. Born on February 25, 1920, Philip Habib became one of the most influential diplomats of his time. The son of Syrian grocers, Habib grew up in Brooklyn, New York, and later attended the University of Idaho. After graduating in 1942, he married and then joined the army, where he served for four years in World War II. Then, while studying for a Ph.D. in economics (which he earned in 1956) from the University of California at Berkeley, Habib began his career in the foreign service, as the third secretary at the U.S. embassy in Canada.

Habib went on to fill various posts in Washington, D.C., and New Zealand, Trinidad, South Korea, and South Vietnam, gaining a reputation as the State Department's foremost expert on Southeast Asia. Under Presidents Johnson and Nixon, he was a key negotiator at the Paris peace talks that ended the Vietnam War. He then served as ambassador to the Republic of Korea and from 1974 was assistant secretary of state, during which time he worked to improve political and economic conditions in war-torn Laos and Cambodia.

In 1976, President Ford named Habib under secretary of state for political affairs, the highest post open to career foreign-service officers, a title he retained under President Carter. As under secretary, Habib arranged a historic meeting between Egyptian president Anwar Sadat and Israeli prime minister Menachem Begin. That meeting produced the 1979 Camp David peace accords between Israel and Egypt, ending more than 20 years of fighting. But before the two countries reached their agreement, Habib suffered a heart attack and decided to retire.

Habib's retirement was to be short-lived. In 1981, President Reagan asked him to help prevent the civil war in Lebanon—in which Israel had interfered—from spreading to the rest of the Middle East. Habib visited leaders in Lebanon, Israel, Syria, and Saudi Arabia to try to negotiate a peace plan and, on July 24, 1981, succeeded in arranging a cease-fire across the Israeli-Lebanese border—a fitting capstone to his lifetime of distinguished diplomacy. Before he died in 1992, Habib received many honors from his colleagues and from the presidents he served.

Another Arab American who has served the U.S. government at the highest levels is Donna Shalala, who in 1992 became secretary of health and human services—the first Arab American to be appointed to a Cabinet position. Born an identical twin on February 14, 1941, Shalala has combined a notable career in education with an impressive series of achievements in the world of government and public affairs.

After graduating in 1962 from Western College for Women in Ohio, Shalala served for two years in the Peace Corps in Iran and then returned to the United States to enter the doctoral program at the Maxwell School of Citizenship and Public Affairs at Syracuse University. After receiving her Ph.D. in 1970, Shalala held a series of teaching positions and fellowships at major institutions such as Columbia University Teachers' College and Yale Law School.

Donna Shalala's expertise in the fields of public policy and educational finance has won her many prestigious posts, including her position as secretary of health and human services.

In 1975, Shalala served as director and treasurer of the Municipal Assistance Corporation (Big Mac), set up to keep New York City from going bankrupt. Big Mac's efforts succeeded, and Shalala accepted a 1977 appointment to the post of assistant secretary for policy development and research at the federal Department of Housing and Urban Development.

In 1980, Shalala became president of Hunter College in New York City. In seven years, she transformed Hunter from a run-down inner-city college into a prestigious institution with a national reputation. Then, in 1988, she became chancellor of the University of Wisconsin at Madison. During her five years at the university, she launched efforts to strengthen undergraduate education and improve opportunities for women and minorities.

Shalala continued to teach during her years at Hunter and Wisconsin. A renowned expert on public policy, urban government, and educational finance, she also served in various capacities on numerous boards and committees, including the American Stock Exchange, the National Women's Law Center, and the Council on Foreign Relations. After her appointment to head the Health and Human Services Department in 1992, she played a central role in President Clinton's efforts to reform the welfare system and improve health care delivery.

Other Arab Americans have made names for themselves as governors, mayors, state legislators, and members of Congress. An American of Syrian descent first was elected to the House of Representatives in 1958, and since then the Arab Americans in Congress have included Senators George Mitchell, Spencer Abraham, James Abourezk, and James Abdnor, as well as Representatives Pat Danner, Nick J. Rahall, and Mary Rose Oakar.

One of the best-known Arab Americans in Washington, D.C., however, is not an officeholder but a reporter. In part, it was her fascination with politics that

Known as the "dean of the White House press corps," Helen Thomas has enjoyed a distinguished career in journalism. Here, she is applauded by President Clinton as she celebrates her birthday in the White House press room.

Boston College's star quarterback Doug Flutie (number 22) won the Heisman Trophy in 1984.

led Helen Thomas into the field of journalism. Born to Syrian immigrant parents and raised in the Arab community of Detroit, Michigan, Thomas graduated in 1942 from Wayne State University in Detroit. She joined the staff of the Washington, D.C., *Daily News* and then took a job in the city room at United Press International (UPI), one of the country's largest wire services. In 1956 she transferred to UPI's national staff, first covering Justice Department news and later reporting on the Department of Health, Education, and Welfare.

Thomas won a White House assignment shortly after the inauguration of President Kennedy in 1961. For the next thirteen years, she followed Presidents

Kennedy, Johnson, Nixon, and Ford to places as far away as China and the Middle East. During this time she married but was widowed shortly thereafter. Becoming UPI's White House bureau chief in 1974, she continued to cover the presidential beat during the Carter, Reagan, Bush, and Clinton administrations. She was the first woman to attain the presidency of the White House Correspondents Association.

Arab Americans have also enjoyed success as athletes. Doug Flutie, for instance, achieved national fame in 1984, when he won the Heisman Trophy, awarded to the best college football player in the United States. While playing quarterback for Boston College, he became the first college football player to pass for more than 10,000 yards. After college, he turned down a Rhodes Scholarship in favor of a million-dollar-a-year contract with the U.S. Football League's New Jersey Generals. Eventually, moving to the Canadian Football League, he became one of that league's leading quarterbacks.

More recently, Lebanese-born Rony Seikaly, who came to the United States to attend Syracuse University, has made a name for himself as a basketball player. In his college career at Syracuse, the 6′11″ Seikaly surpassed 1,000 points and 1,000 rebounds. Since entering the National Basketball Association in 1988, he has established himself as one of the league's finer centers.

In the world of entertainment, a number of Arab Americans stand out. Casey Kasem, one of America's most familiar voices, has been a nationally syndicated broadcasting personality since 1970. He currently hosts four radio shows: "Casey's Top 40," "Casey's Countdown for Adult Contemporary," "Casey's Hot 20," and "Casey's Biggest Hits." His parents, Druze immigrants who operated a grocery store in Detroit, named him Kamal Amin Kasem at his birth in 1932. The first disc jockey to receive a star on Hollywood Boulevard's Walk of Fame, Kasem was the youngest person ever inducted into the National Association of Broadcasters Radio Hall of Fame. An activist in social causes, Kasem raised funds for the restoration of the Statue of Liberty and campaigned against the stereotyping of Arabs during the 1991 Persian Gulf War.

Other well-known Arab Americans in entertainment have included F. Murray Abraham, who starred in the 1985 movie *Amadeus* and won the Oscar for best actor; musician/composer Frank Zappa and his children Moon Unit and Dweezil; singers Paula Abdul, Paul Anka, and Tiny Tim; actor Jamie Farr; and actor/comedian Danny Thomas, along with his daughter Marlo Thomas.

In other fields, Arab Americans of note include Candy Lightner, the founder of Mothers Against Drunk Driving (MADD); Paul Orfalea, founder and chairman of the Kinko's chain of copying and printing stores; Michael DeBakey, pioneering heart surgeon; and General George Joulwan, who headed NATO during the first part of that organization's mission in Bosnia in the 1990s. Christa McAuliffe, the "teacher in space" who perished on the *Challenger* shuttle in 1985, was also an Arab American.

Thousands of other Arab Americans, though not famous, successfully pursue careers in the sciences, the arts, business, politics, and education. They live in every state and have thoroughly assimilated into American culture.

Toward a Brighter Future

Despite the success of Arab Americans, they have confronted a growing problem of anti-Arab discrimination. Several factors, primarily the situation in the Middle East, have generated a significant amount of anti-Arab sentiment in North America in recent years. During the 1991 Persian Gulf War, for example, various Arab-American organizations received threats.

Arab Americans suffer most when Arab terrorist activity flares up abroad. In at least one such incident,

Candy Lightner continued the tradition of Arab-American community involvement by founding Mothers Against Drunk Driving (MADD).

Casey Kasem, a nationally syndicated broadcaster since 1970, has introduced many new stars to music listeners.

an Arab American was killed. In October 1985, Alex Odeh, the regional director of the American-Arab Anti-Discrimination Committee in Southern California, died at the hands of unidentified terrorists. The attack followed Odeh's statement to the press that the Palestine Liberation Organization had not been involved in the hijacking of the Italian cruise ship *Achille Lauro*. Odeh also denounced all terrorism, but this part of his statement was not broadcast. The next day, Odeh was killed by a bomb wired to the front door of his office building.

As Odeh's tragedy illustrates, the frequent media coverage of terrorist violence may in some cases encourage non-Arabs to vent their anger on innocent Arab Americans. Highly visible Arab-American communities bear the brunt of these attacks and at times feel under siege by anti-Arab hate mongers. Television shows, movies, and political cartoons depicting Arabs as treacherous and fanatical have an equally bad effect.

In response, the diverse Arab-American community has developed a greater political cohesiveness. Today, many Arab individuals and organizations campaign for international peacekeeping efforts in the Middle East. They also do everything they can to promote good relations between the United States and the countries of the Arab world, as well as between themselves and other groups of Americans.

Academy Award–winning actor F. Murray Abraham is one of the many famous Arab Americans in the entertainment world.

Proud of their Arab heritage, Arab Americans are patriotic citizens of the United States.

The situation in the Middle East will no doubt continue to trouble Arab Americans. Deeply proud of both their ancestral culture and their American heritage, Arab Americans hope to encourage understanding in their fellow Americans. They dream of a day when the United States will have harmonious relations with the Arab states. They also hope for a future in which their success in America will be complemented by peace and prosperity in the world they left behind.

FURTHER READING

Abraham, Nabeel. "Arab Americans." *Gale Encyclopedia of Multicultural America*. Detroit: Gale Research, 1995.

American-Arab Anti-Discrimination Committee. World Wide Web home page at http://www.adc.org.

Benough, W. "The Foreign Element in New York, a Syrian Colony." *Harper's*, August 3, 1985.

CaféArabica: The Arab-American Online Community Center. World Wide Web home page at http://www.cafearabica.com.

Cristgau, Alice E. *The Laugh Peddler*. New York: Young Scott Books, 1968.

El-Badry, Samia. "The Arab-Americans." *American Demographics*, January 1994.

Hagopian, Elaine C., and Ann Paden, eds. *The Arab-Americans: Studies in Assimilation*. Wilmette, IL: Medina University Press International, 1969.

Hitti, Philip K. *Syrians in America*. New York: George Doran, 1924.

Kayal, Philip and Joseph. *Syrian Lebanese in America: A Study in Religion and Assimilation*. Boston: Twayne, 1975.

McCarus, Ernest, ed. *The Development of Arab-American Identity*. Ann Arbor: University of Michigan Press, 1994.

Naff, Alixa. "Arabs." *Harvard Encyclopedia of American Ethnic Groups*. Cambridge, MA: Harvard University Press, 1980.

————. *Becoming American: The Early Arab Immigrant Experience*. Carbondale: Southern Illinois University Press, 1985.

National Association of Arab Americans. World Wide Web home page at http://www.steele.com/naaa/.

INDEX

Abraham, 19
Abraham, F. Murray, 102, 104
Addes, George, 75–76
Al-Bayan, 77
Aleppo, 18
Algeria, 13
Al-Hikma, 22
Al-Hoda, 77
Allah, 20
American Arab Anti-Discrimination
    Committee, 91, 103
American University of Beirut, 25, 59
Arab Americans
    classified incorrectly, 14
    discrimination and violence against,
        102–105
    education level of second wave
        immigrants, 85, 87–89
    effect of assimilation on traditional
        values, 65–69, 72–74, 82–83
    establishment of Arab-American
        churches, 59–60, 72–74
    first wave of immigration, 13–14,
        31–33
    in garment industry, 62–64
    geographic dispersal in United
        States, 45, 47
    newspapers, 76–82, 90
    as peddlers, 38–45
    population, 13
    restrictions placed on immigration,
        33
    second wave of immigration, 15,
        85–93
    as shopkeepers, 60–61
Arab-American Institute, 91
Arabian Nights, 24
Arabian Peninsula, 13, 18–19, 22, 24
Arabian Sea, 18
Arabic language, 13, 19, 22–23, 25, 73,
    92–93
Arab-Israeli War, 15
Arab League, 86–87
Arabs
    agriculture and, 17
    creation of Arab Empire, 22–24
    definition of, 13

development of oil reserves,
    28–29
and European colonialism,
    25–26, 29
history, 18–29
importance of Islam, 20–22
and Israel, 27–28
nomadic culture of, 17
scientific and cultural
    achievements, 23–24
Araq, 48
Arbeely, Ibrahim, 77
Arbeely, Najib, 77
Association of Arab American
    University Graduates, 91
Assyrians, 19
Atlantic Monthly, 95
Atlantic Ocean, 18
Austria-Hungary, 25
Azar, Raymond S., 61

Babylonians, 19
Baghdad, 24
Bahrain, 13
Balfour Declaration, 26
Begin, Menachem, 97
Beirut, 25
Blake, William, 79
Boston, 47, 76, 79
Byzantium, 23

Cairo, 18, 24
Carter, Jimmy, 97, 101
Cedar Rapids, 47
Chicago, 47, 82
China, 22
Christgau, Alice E., 41
Christian Science Monitor, 95
Columbus, Christopher, 31
Cordoba, 24

Dallas, 62
Damascus, 18
Daughters of Syria, 59
Dearborn, 45, 89
Druze, 21–22, 33, 45, 68, 73

PICTURE CREDITS

We would like to thank the following sources for providing photographs: ABC/Watermark: p. 103; AP/Wide World Photos: pp. 94, 98, 102; Art Resource/Bildarchiv Foto Marburg: p. 23; Millard Berry: pp. 84–85, 88, 89; The Bettmann Archive: pp. 16–17, 21, 81; British Museum. Photograph by Peter Clayton: p. 18; Cedar Rapids Islamic Center and Mosque: p. 73; Culver Pictures: p. 39; Freer Gallery of Art, Washington, D.C.: p. 22; J. M. Haggar: Photo courtesy of the Institute of Texas Cultures: p. 63; Library of Congress: pp. 25, 32, 35, 36, 60, 77, 78; Middle East Photo, Paterson, N.J.: pp. 87, 92; Dr. Rosa Lee Nemir: p. 82; New York Public Library Picture Collection: p. 20; Popperfoto/Archive Photos: p. 104; Reuters/Bettmann Newsphotos: p. 86; Reuters/Gary Cameron/Archive Photos: p. 99; Reuters/David Silverman/Archive Photos: p. 29; Edward Schaded and the Institute of Texas Cultures: p. 12; Smithsonian Institution, Washington, D.C.: pp. 30, 40, 43, 45, 46, 48, 56, 58, 64, 66, 67, 68, 70, 72, 74, 75; Mark Stein Studios: p. 24; Katrina Thomas: pp. 49, 50 (top), 50 (bottom), 51 (top), 51 (bottom), 52, 53 (top), 53 (bottom), 54, 55 (top), 55 (bottom), 56, 90, 91; United Nations: pp. 26, 27, 28; UPI/Bettmann Newsphotos: pp. 93, 96, 100, 105.

ALIXA NAFF, an Arab American, is a scholar of Middle Eastern social and political history with a special interest in the history of Arab immigration to the United States. Her book, *Becoming American, the Early Arab Immigrant Experience,* was published in 1985. Her articles include the entry on Arab Americans in the *Harvard Encyclopedia of American Ethnic Groups.*

DANIEL PATRICK MOYNIHAN is the senior United States senator from New York. He is also the only person in American history to serve in the cabinets or subcabinets of four successive presidents—Kennedy, Johnson, Nixon, and Ford. Formerly a professor of government at Harvard University, he has written and edited many books, including *Beyond the Melting Pot, Ethnicity: Theory and Experience* (both with Nathan Glazer), *Loyalties,* and *Family and Nation.*

CENTRAL MIDDLE SCHOOL
MEDIA CENTER